WORDPERFECT 7 FOR WINDOWS® FOR DUMMIES®

Quick Reference

by Greg Harvey

IDG Books Worldwide, Inc.
An International Data Group Company

Foster City, CA ✦ Chicago, IL ✦ Indianapolis, IN ✦ New York, NY

WordPerfect® 9 For Windows® For Dummies® Quick Reference

Published by
IDG Books Worldwide, Inc.
An International Data Group Company
919 E. Hillsdale Blvd.
Suite 400
Foster City, CA 94404
www.idgbooks.com (IDG Books Worldwide Web site)
www.dummies.com (Dummies Press Web site)

Copyright © 1999 IDG Books Worldwide, Inc. All rights reserved. No part of this book, including interior design, cover design, and icons, may be reproduced or transmitted in any form, by any means (electronic, photocopying, recording, or otherwise) without the prior written permission of the publisher.

Library of Congress Catalog Card No.: 99-63102

ISBN: 0-7645-0428-2

Printed in the United States of America

10 9 8 7 6 5 4 3 2 1

1P/QR/QW/ZZ/IN

Distributed in the United States by IDG Books Worldwide, Inc.

Distributed by CDG Books Canada Inc. for Canada; by Transworld Publishers Limited in the United Kingdom; by IDG Norge Books for Norway; by IDG Sweden Books for Sweden; by Woodslane Pty. Ltd. for Australia; by Woodslane (NZ) Ltd. for New Zealand; by TransQuest Publishers Pte Ltd. for Singapore, Malaysia, Thailand, Indonesia, and Hong Kong; by ICG Muse, Inc. for Japan; by Norma Comunicaciones S.A. for Colombia; by Intersoft for South Africa; by Le Monde en Tique for France; by International Thomson Publishing for Germany, Austria and Switzerland; by Distribuidora Cuspide for Argentina; by Livraria Cultura for Brazil; by Ediciones ZETA S.C.R. Ltda. for Peru; by WS Computer Publishing Corporation, Inc., for the Philippines; by Contemporanea de Ediciones for Venezuela; by Express Computer Distributors for the Caribbean and West Indies; by Micronesia Media Distributor, Inc. for Micronesia; by Grupo Editorial Norma S.A. for Guatemala; by Chips Computadoras S.A. de C.V. for Mexico; by Editorial Norma de Panama S.A. for Panama; by American Bookshops for Finland. Authorized Sales Agent: Anthony Rudkin Associates for the Middle East and North Africa.

For general information on IDG Books Worldwide's books in the U.S., please call our Consumer Customer Service department at 800-762-2974. For reseller information, including discounts and premium sales, please call our Reseller Customer Service department at 800-434-3422.

For information on where to purchase IDG Books Worldwide's books outside the U.S., please contact our International Sales department at 317-596-5530 or fax 317-596-5692.

For consumer information on foreign language translations, please contact our Customer Service department at 1-800-434-3422, fax 317-596-5692, or e-mail rights@idgbooks.com.

For information on licensing foreign or domestic rights, please phone +1-650-655-3109.

For sales inquiries and special prices for bulk quantities, please contact our Sales department at 650-655-3200 or write to the address above.

For information on using IDG Books Worldwide's books in the classroom or for ordering examination copies, please contact our Educational Sales department at 800-434-2086 or fax 317-596-5499.

For press review copies, author interviews, or other publicity information, please contact our Public Relations department at 650-655-3000 or fax 650-655-3299.

For authorization to photocopy items for corporate, personal, or educational use, please contact Copyright Clearance Center, 222 Rosewood Drive, Danvers, MA 01923, or fax 978-750-4470.

LIMIT OF LIABILITY/DISCLAIMER OF WARRANTY: THE PUBLISHER AND AUTHOR HAVE USED THEIR BEST EFFORTS IN PREPARING THIS BOOK. THE PUBLISHER AND AUTHOR MAKE NO REPRESENTATIONS OR WARRANTIES WITH RESPECT TO THE ACCURACY OR COMPLETENESS OF THE CONTENTS OF THIS BOOK AND SPECIFICALLY DISCLAIM ANY IMPLIED WARRANTIES OF MERCHANTABILITY OR FITNESS FOR A PARTICULAR PURPOSE. THERE ARE NO WARRANTIES WHICH EXTEND BEYOND THE DESCRIPTIONS CONTAINED IN THIS PARAGRAPH. NO WARRANTY MAY BE CREATED OR EXTENDED BY SALES REPRESENTATIVES OR WRITTEN SALES MATERIALS. THE ACCURACY AND COMPLETENESS OF THE INFORMATION PROVIDED HEREIN AND THE OPINIONS STATED HEREIN ARE NOT GUARANTEED OR WARRANTED TO PRODUCE ANY PARTICULAR RESULTS, AND THE ADVICE AND STRATEGIES CONTAINED HEREIN MAY NOT BE SUITABLE FOR EVERY INDIVIDUAL. NEITHER THE PUBLISHER NOR AUTHOR SHALL BE LIABLE FOR ANY LOSS OF PROFIT OR ANY OTHER COMMERCIAL DAMAGES, INCLUDING BUT NOT LIMITED TO SPECIAL, INCIDENTAL, CONSEQUENTIAL, OR OTHER DAMAGES.

Trademarks: All brand names and product names used in this book are trade names, service marks, trademarks, or registered trademarks of their respective owners. IDG Books Worldwide is not associated with any product or vendor mentioned in this book.

 is a registered trademark or trademark under exclusive license to IDG Books Worldwide, Inc. from International Data Group, Inc. in the United States and/or other countries.

About the Author

Greg Harvey, the author of more than 75 computer books (and he just keeps on going and going and going), has been training businesspeople in the use of DOS, Windows, and software applications programs, such as Word, Excel, WordPerfect, Lotus 1-2-3, and dBASE, since 1983. He has written numerous training manuals, user guides, and books for business users of software. Harvey is the author of *Excel 2000 For Windows For Dummies, 1-2-3 For Dummies, PC World WordPerfect 6 Handbook, DOS For Dummies Quick Reference, WordPerfect 8 For Windows For Dummies Quick Reference,* and *Windows 98 For Dummies Quick Reference,* all from IDG Books Worldwide, Inc.

Greg Harvey is a product of the great American Midwest, born in the Chicagoland area in 1949 in the dark ages of the Cold War before the time of McDonald's, MTV, and, certainly, personal computers. On the shores of Lake Michigan, he learned his letters and numbers and showed great promise in the world of academia.

In 1966 (ah, the sixties), he entered the University of Illinois at Urbana, where he was greatly influenced by such deep philosophers as Abbie Hoffman and Mahatma Gandhi. At the beginning of 1971, Greg migrated West from Chicago to San Francisco (with flowers in his hair). Deciding it was high time to get a skill so that he could find a real job, he enrolled in the Drafting and Design program at Laney College in Oakland, and then spent nine years working over a hot drafting table.

In 1981, Greg went back to school at San Francisco State University, this time to earn his secondary teaching credential. Upon completion of his teacher training, he bought one of the very first IBM personal computers (with 16K and a single 160K floppy disk!). He still vividly remembers pouring over the premier issue of *PC World* for every piece of information that could teach him how to make peace with his blankety-blank personal computer.

After a few high-tech jobs in Silicon Valley, Greg turned to software training to gain, as he put it, "the perspective of the poor schmoe at the end of the terminal." During the next three years, Greg trained business users of all skill levels for several major independent software training companies in the San Francisco Bay area on a whole plethora of software programs. In the fall of 1986, he hooked up with Sybex, a local computer book publisher, for whom he wrote the computer training book, *Mastering SuperCalc.* And the rest, as they say, is history.

Currently, he operates a multimedia company called MIND over media, Inc. To get in touch with him, send your fan e-mail to gharvey@mindovermedia.com **or visit the MIND over media Web site at** http://www.mindovermedia.com.

ABOUT IDG BOOKS WORLDWIDE

Welcome to the world of IDG Books Worldwide.

IDG Books Worldwide, Inc., is a subsidiary of International Data Group, the world's largest publisher of computer-related information and the leading global provider of information services on information technology. IDG was founded more than 30 years ago by Patrick J. McGovern and now employs more than 9,000 people worldwide. IDG publishes more than 290 computer publications in over 75 countries. More than 90 million people read one or more IDG publications each month.

Launched in 1990, IDG Books Worldwide is today the #1 publisher of best-selling computer books in the United States. We are proud to have received eight awards from the Computer Press Association in recognition of editorial excellence and three from Computer Currents' First Annual Readers' Choice Awards. Our best-selling ...*For Dummies*® series has more than 50 million copies in print with translations in 31 languages. IDG Books Worldwide, through a joint venture with IDG's Hi-Tech Beijing, became the first U.S. publisher to publish a computer book in the People's Republic of China. In record time, IDG Books Worldwide has become the first choice for millions of readers around the world who want to learn how to better manage their businesses.

Our mission is simple: Every one of our books is designed to bring extra value and skill-building instructions to the reader. Our books are written by experts who understand and care about our readers. The knowledge base of our editorial staff comes from years of experience in publishing, education, and journalism — experience we use to produce books to carry us into the new millennium. In short, we care about books, so we attract the best people. We devote special attention to details such as audience, interior design, use of icons, and illustrations. And because we use an efficient process of authoring, editing, and desktop publishing our books electronically, we can spend more time ensuring superior content and less time on the technicalities of making books.

You can count on our commitment to deliver high-quality books at competitive prices on topics you want to read about. At IDG Books W
quality for more than 30 years. You'll find no better book on a subject than one from IDG Books Worldwide.

orldwide, we continue in the IDG tradition of delivering

John Kilcullen
Chairman and CEO
IDG Books Worldwide, Inc.

Steven Berkowitz
President and Publisher
IDG Books Worldwide, Inc.

Eighth Annual
Computer Press
Awards ≥1992

Ninth Annual
Computer Press
Awards ≥1993

Tenth Annual
Computer Press
Awards ≥1994

Eleventh Annual
Computer Press
Awards ≥1995

IDG is the world's leading IT media, research and exposition company. Founded in 1964, IDG had 1997 revenues of $2.05 billion and has more than 9,000 employees worldwide. IDG offers the widest range of media options that reach IT buyers in 75 countries representing 95% of worldwide IT spending. IDG's diverse product and services portfolio spans six key areas including print publishing, online publishing, expositions and conferences, market research, education and training, and global marketing services. More than 90 million people read one or more of IDG's 290 magazines and newspapers, including IDG's leading global brands — Computerworld, PC World, Network World, Macworld and the Channel World family of publications. IDG Books Worldwide is one of the fastest-growing computer book publishers in the world, with more than 700 titles in 36 languages. The "...For Dummies®" series alone has more than 50 million copies in print. IDG offers online users the largest network of technology-specific Web sites around the world through IDG.net (http://www.idg.net), which comprises more than 225 targeted Web sites in 55 countries worldwide. International Data Corporation (IDC) is the world's largest provider of information technology data, analysis and consulting, with research centers in over 41 countries and more than 400 research analysts worldwide. IDG World Expo is a leading producer of more than 168 globally branded conferences and expositions in 35 countries including E3 (Electronic Entertainment Expo), Macworld Expo, ComNet, Windows World Expo, ICE (Internet Commerce Expo), Agenda, DEMO, and Spotlight. IDG's training subsidiary, ExecuTrain, is the world's largest computer training company, with more than 230 locations worldwide and 785 training courses. IDG Marketing Services helps industry-leading IT companies build international brand recognition by developing global integrated marketing programs via IDG's print, online and exposition products worldwide. Further information about the company can be found at www.idg.com. 1/24/99

Dedication

To Michael Bryant and family — Melinda (Mel), Marla (Sachiko), Mike (Keichi), and Kinna — for all their love and support through the years.

Author's Acknowledgments

I want to thank the following people, who worked so hard to make this book a reality: David Solomon and John Kilcullen, for their support for this "baby" ...*For Dummies* book.

Brandon Nordin and Milissa Koloski, for coming up with the original concept of quick references for the rest of us.

Joyce Pepple for her help in getting this edition underway and keeping it on track.

Andrea Boucher, Melba Hopper, and Stacey Mickelbart for their editorial assistance.

Lee Musick, for the technical review, and the staff in IDG Books Worldwide's Production department.

Michael Bryant, for his marvelous job in taking the text from WordPerfect Version 6.1 all the way to Version 9. (A hundred thousand thanks!)

Lorenzo Levinger, Matt Gallagher, and Christopher Aiken, for proofreading the lovely prose and retaking all those wonderful screen shots. (Way to go, guys!)

Last, but never least, I want to acknowledge my indebtedness to Dan Gookin, whose vision, sardonic wit, and (sometimes) good humor produced *DOS For Dummies,* the "Mother" of all ...*For Dummies* books. Thanks for the inspiration and the book that made it all possible, Dan.

Greg Harvey

Inverness, California

Publisher's Acknowledgments

We're proud of this book; please register your comments through our IDG Books Worldwide Online Registration Form located at: http://my2cents.dummies.com.

Some of the people who helped bring this book to market include the following:

Acquisitions, Editorial, and Media Development

Project Editors: Andrea C. Boucher, Tim Gallan, Melba D. Hopper

Acquisitions Editor: Joyce Pepple

Technical Editor: Lee Musick

Editorial Manager: Mary Corder

Editorial Assistant: Paul Kuzmic

Production

Associate Project Coordinator: Maridee Ennis

Layout and Graphics: Angie Hunckler, Anna Rohrer, Brent Savage, Janet Seib, Michael A. Sullivan, Brian Torwelle

Proofreaders: Arielle Carole Mennelle, Nancy Price, Marianne Santy, Ethel M. Winslow

Indexer: Johnna VanHoose

Special Help: Valery Bourke, Kathleen Dobie, Steven H. Hayes, Donna Love, Rev Mengle, Stacey Mickelbart, Rowena Rappaport

---

General and Administrative

IDG Books Worldwide, Inc: John Kilcullen, CEO; Steven Berkowitz, President and Publisher

IDG Books Technology Publishing: Brenda McLaughlin, Senior Vice President and Group Publisher

Dummies Technology Press and Dummies Editorial: Diane Graves Steele, Vice President and Associate Publisher; Mary Bednarek, Director of Acquisitions and Product Development; Kristin A. Cocks, Editorial Director

Dummies Trade Press: Kathleen A. Welton, Vice President and Publisher; Kevin Thornton, Acquisitions Manager

IDG Books Production for Dummies Press: Michael R. Britton, Vice President of Production and Creative Services; Cindy L. Phipps, Manager of Project Coordination, Production Proofreading, and Indexing; Shelley Lea, Supervisor of Graphics and Design; Debbie J. Gates, Production Systems Specialist; Robert Springer, Supervisor of Proofreading; Debbie Stailey, Production Control Manager; Tony Augsburger, Supervisor of Reprints and Bluelines

Dummies Packaging and Book Design: Patty Page, Manager, Promotions Marketing

◆

The publisher would like to give special thanks to Patrick J. McGovern, without whom this book would not have been possible.

◆

Contents at a Glance

Introduction 1

Part I: Getting to Know WordPerfect 9 5

Part II: Setting Up and Editing a Document 21

Part III: Formatting Documents and Text 61

Part IV: Printing Your Documents 89

Part V: Making Your Work Go Faster 105

Part VI: Desktop Publishing 137

Part VII: Web Publishing 157

Part VIII: Potpourri 171

Glossary 189

Index 195

Book Registration Information .... Back of Book

Table of Contents

Introduction 1
- What's in This Book 2
- The Cast of Icons 3
- Conventions Used in This Book 3
- Feedback, Baby 3

Part I: Getting to Know WordPerfect 9 5
- Your Basic Document 6
- All Kinds of Cursors 6
- Running 'Round the Keyboard 7
- Mousing Around 9
- Using Menus 10
  - Take the shortcut keys 11
  - QuickMenus 12
- Carrying On with a Dialog Box 13
- The WordPerfect 9 Window and Its Parts 14
- ¶ Is for Paragraph 17
- Starting WordPerfect 9 17

Part II: Setting Up and Editing a Document 21
- Border/Fill 22
- Cancel 23
- Close (Document) 23
- Convert Case 24
- Cut, Copy, and Paste 24
  - Do you wanna move or copy? 24
  - A few caveats 25
- Delete (Text) 25
- Document Information 26
- Document Summary 26
- Draft View 26
- Drag and Drop (Text) 27
- Exit WordPerfect 27
- Find and Replace 27
- Footnotes and Endnotes 29
  - Creating a footnote or endnote 29
  - Editing text in a footnote or endnote 30
  - Changing the footnote or endnote numbering ... 30
- Grammatik 31
- Header/Footer 31
- Help 33

Hyphenation 35
Insertion Point 37
Line Spacing 38
New (Document) 38
    Opening a new document 38
    Selecting a template for the new document 39
Open (Document) 40
Page Borders 41
Page Break 42
Page Numbering 42
Page View 43
Paragraph Borders 43
PerfectExpert 44
Properties 45
Save 47
    Saving a file for the first time 47
    Embedded fonts 49
    Saving a file on subsequent occasions 49
Save As 49
Select (Text) 51
    Natural selection 51
    The QuickMenu method 51
    Other slick ways to extend a block 51
Show ¶ 52
Spell Check 53
Thesaurus 53
Two Page View 53
Undo 54
Window 55
Writing Tools 55
    Spell checking a document 56
    Using Grammatik 57
    Using Thesaurus 59
Zoom 60

Part III: Formatting Documents and Text 61

Bold 62
Bullets and Numbers 62
    Bullets and numbers in a snap 62
    Getting rid of those bullets 63
Center Line 64
Center Page 64
Columns 65
    Creating columns 65
    Moving through columns 66
Double Indent 67

Table of Contents

Drop Cap 68
    Dropping caps with the pros 68
    Customizing drop caps 68
Flush Right 69
Font 70
    Using the "Font Properties" dialog box 70
    Turning everything off! 73
    RealTime Preview 73
Hanging Indent 74
Indent 75
Justification 76
Line Numbering 76
Margins 78
Outline 78
    Creating an outline 79
    Using the Outline Property Bar 80
Redline/Strikeout 81
Ruler Bar 82
    Clicking ruler parts 82
    Using the margin icons and tab stops 82
Styles 83
    Styles à la QuickStyle 83
    Turning on a style before you type the text 84
    Turning off the style in a new paragraph 84
    Applying a paragraph style to an
      existing paragraph of text 85
Typeover 87
Underline 87
WordPerfect Characters 87

Part IV: Printing Your Documents 89

Envelope 90
Insert Filename 91
Labels 91
    Mass quantities of labels 92
    Editing labels in the document window 93
Merge 93
    Creating a table data file 93
    Creating a form file 96
    Merging the data and form file 98
    Envelopes and labels 99
Page Size 99
Print 101

Part V: Making Your Work Go Faster 105

Application Bar 106
Auto Scroll 107
Bookmark 108
    Creating a bookmark 108
    Finding a bookmark 109
    Using a QuickMark 109
    Setting a QuickMark 109
    Finding a QuickMark 109
DAD (Desktop Applications Director) 110
    Let's add to DAD 110
    How to get rid of DAD 110
    How to get DAD started 111
Date/Time 111
    Inserting the date as text 111
    Inserting the date as a secret code 112
Dragon NaturallySpeaking 112
    Take this down 113
    A word to the wise 114
    New words in the document 114
    Show me what you know 115
Go To 116
Grammar-As-You-Go 116
Hide Bars 116
Macros 117
    Recording macros 117
    Playing back macros 119
    Attaching your macro to the document template 119
Prompt-As-You-Go 120
Proofread 120
Property Bar 122
    The buttons on the Property bar 122
    Featuring the Property bar 123
    Creating a full-length feature 123
QuickCorrect 125
QuickFinder 126
    QuickFinder Searcher 126
    QuickFinder Manager 128
QuickFormat 129
QuickMark 130
QuickMenu 130
QuickWords 130
    Creating QuickWords 131
    Using QuickWords 132
Repeat 132

Table of Contents

Shadow Cursor (The Shadow
 [Cursor] Knows) 133
  Using the shadow cursor..133
  Configuring the shadow cursor 133
  Turning the shadow cursor off and on 133
Spell-As-You-Go 134
Status Bar 134
Toolbars 134
  Show me the toolbars! 134
  Button up that toolbar! 134
  Create a custom toolbar 136

Part VI: Desktop Publishing 137

Advance 138
Block Protect 138
Conditional End of Page 138
Graphics (Boxes) 138
  Getting graphic 139
  Little boxes with style 139
  Moving and sizing graphics boxes 141
  Editing graphics 141
Guidelines 142
Keep Text Together 142
Line Height 143
Make It Fit 144
Paragraph Format 145
Reference 146
Shapes 149
Sort 150
  It takes all sorts 150
  Sorting out the sorts 151
Tables 152
  Creating a table 152
  Entering text in a table 153
  Skewed table cells 153
  Turn off skewing 154
Typesetting 155
Watermarks 155
Widow/Orphan 156

Part VII: Web Publishing 157

Hyperlink 158
  Creating a hyperlink 158
  Editing a hyperlink 159
  Using SpeedLinks 159
Internet Publisher 160
  Creating a new Web page 161
  Adding graphics to a Web page 162

      Creating a table on the Web page 163
      Adding lists to the Web page 163
      Inserting horizontal rules in the Web page 165
      Adding a form to the Web page 165
      Viewing the Web document in a browser 166
      Converting a WordPerfect document
         into a Web page 167
      Saving the converted Web page 168
  SpeedLinks 169
  Web Page View 170

Part VIII: Potpourri 171

  Address Book 172
      Creating an address book 172
      Messing with your address book 173
  Bar Code 174
  Character Map 175
  Comments 175
      Creating a comment 175
      Editing a comment 176
  Document 176
      Comparing documents 177
      Master/subdocuments 178
      Using a master document 178
  Equation 179
  Highlight 179
  Language 180
  Master Document 181
  Paste Special 181
  Reveal Codes 182
      Revealing the codes 182
      Using Reveal Codes 182
  Sound 184
      What's that sound? 184
      Recording a sound 185
      Adding a sound clip to your document 185
  Spreadsheet/Database 186
  WordPerfect Office 2000 187
      How suite it is 187
      Using WordPerfect Office 2000 187

Glossary: Techie Talk 189

Index 195

Book Registration Information .... Back of Book

How to Use This Book

You have all heard of online help. Well, just think of this book as on-side help. Keep it by your side when you're at the computer, and before you try to use a WordPerfect command that you're the least bit unsure of, look up the command in the appropriate section. Scan the entry and follow the step-by-step procedures to quickly become acquainted with the feature.

This little book can't cover every single feature in WordPerfect 9, but it does show you how to do all of the basics and a lot of complicated stuff, too.

2 How to Use This Book

What's in This Book

As a means of ferreting out the best possible paths to all the commands, features, and functions in WordPerfect for Windows, I offer you the *WordPerfect 9 For Windows For Dummies Quick Reference*. This book not only gives you the lowdown on WordPerfect commands, but it also demonstrates how to harness the power of WordPerfect 9 so that you will automatically be elevated to the lofty position of WordPerfect 9 Guru of the Office. For your convenience, this book is divided into eight parts and a glossary. Each part deals with a specific area in the world of word processing so that you can zero in on a problem or question with the greatest of ease. In each part, you find references to WordPerfect 9 menu commands in alphabetical order with a short description of the command's usage, followed by step-by-step procedures for accomplishing many everyday tasks. Along the way, I'll give you lots of tips and ways to speed up your work. Here's what's in the parts:

- ✦ Part I explains word processing basics and shows you how to start up WordPerfect.
- ✦ Part II helps you set up and edit the text within a document.
- ✦ Part III deals with all aspects of formatting.
- ✦ Part IV tells you everything you need to know about printing.
- ✦ Part V is filled with shortcuts and tips that will make you a more efficient WordPerfect user.
- ✦ Part VI shows you how to use WordPerfect's desktop publishing tools so that you can give your documents a professional look.
- ✦ Part VII covers the task of converting your documents into HTML-based files for Web publishing.
- ✦ Part VIII has some fun and useful information that didn't fit anywhere else.
- ✦ The Glossary defines some computing and word processing terms.

The Cast of Icons

In your travels with the WordPerfect 9 for Windows commands in this book, you'll come across the following icons:

Something brand-new in Version 9 of WordPerfect for Windows.

A tip to make you a more clever WordPerfect user.

Look out! There's some little something in this command that can get you into trouble.

As always in Windows programs, there are numerous ways to do the same thing. Features flagged with this icon are certified *muy rapido*.

A handy-dandy pointer to the sections in *WordPerfect 9 For Windows For Dummies* where you can find more examples of how to do something.

Conventions Used in This Book

When I refer to a toolbar button, I often place a picture of it in the left margin.

When referring to menu commands, I do something like this:

File➪Open

This means choose the Open command from the File menu. The underlined characters indicate that you can use an Alt-key combination to access the command. In this case, Alt+F+O initiates the Open command.

Feedback, Baby

My goal is to give you, dear reader, a useful quick reference for learning the many features in WordPerfect 9. While I've put quite a few tips and tricks into this little compendium, I'm sure there are many more to be discovered. Feel free to drop me a line via e-mail at gharvey@mindovermedia.com and share any nuggets you find as you master WordPerfect 9. Your comments are also welcome. As any self-respecting Hendrix fan knows, I love feedback.

4 How to Use This Book

Part I

Getting to Know WordPerfect 9

The great success of the ...*For Dummies* book series is largely due to the legions of computer newbies who discover a real need to make use of that big box with the mouse thing sitting in the middle of the desk. Though they may not know the difference between a word processor and a food processor, darn it, they do know what learning takes. If you're among this group of intrepid souls, Part I of this book is just the ticket. I explain the secrets of funny-sounding words like *cursor, scroll,* and *double-click* and how to work magic with a mouse. Of course, if you're already a proclaimed wizard around the office as well as in the kitchen, skip ahead to Part II to discover why WordPerfect 9 for Windows is such a cool word processor.

In this part . . .

- What is a document?
- The cursor, the keyboard, and the mouse
- The meaning of menus
- Doing dialog boxes
- Getting started in WordPerfect 9

Your Basic Document

All word processors start you out with a blank document, and WordPerfect 9 is no different. You may be typing a letter, report, memo, or even screenplay, but to the computer it remains a document.

When you first crank up WordPerfect, you get a new document with the generic name Document1 (unmodified) displayed in the title bar at the very top of the screen. If you want another new document, click the New Blank Document button on the WordPerfect 9 toolbar and you receive Document2 (unmodified). The unmodified portion of the generic name disappears after you strike your first key indicating that you have indeed modified the document. If you keep clicking the New Blank Document button, you get more sequentially numbered generic documents. Although this phenomenon is mildly amusing at first, the real fun begins after you save the document and give it a name you can live with.

To save and name your generic document, just click the Save button on the WordPerfect 9 toolbar to open the "Save File" dialog box shown in the following figure. If you type **My Memo** in the "File name" text box, WordPerfect renames the generic document MY MEMO.WPD. The *.WPD* tacked onto the name is the file extension that lets you and the computer know that MY MEMO is a WordPerfect document. You can get more info on setting up documents in Part II.

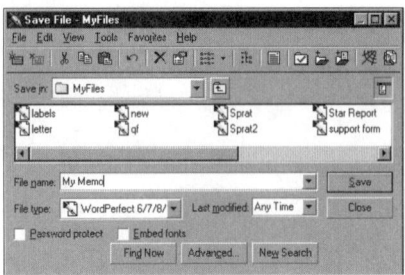

All Kinds of Cursors

Cursors appear in many forms on the computer screen and serve two very basic functions. They let you know where you are on-screen or what the computer is doing. The following table shows the cursors you see most often while working in WordPerfect (or any other Windows 95 or 98 program, for that matter).

Running 'Round the Keyboard   7

Cursor	Name	What It Does
I	Insertion point	Blinks on and off to show your place in the document. All actions take place at the insertion point. Text appears at the insertion point when you begin typing. When you paste items from the Clipboard, they appear at the insertion point.
I / ↖	Mouse cursor	Also known as a mouse pointer, this cursor moves around the computer screen as you move the mouse. When the cursor is in the document window, it looks like the end view of an I-beam. To enter text in a new place, move the I-beam cursor to the new location, click, and start typing. When the cursor passes over something you can select, like a menu item or toolbar button, it turns into a white arrow. Click with the white arrow pointer to select the menu item or tool.
⌛	Busy cursor	When you ask WordPerfect to perform a really major task, an hourglass appears on-screen to let you know that something is happening, even though the opposite seems more apparent.
↖?	Help cursor	If you are curious about some feature in a WordPerfect 9 window, press Shift+F1, and the mouse pointer changes to an arrow with a little question mark beside it. At this point, you can click any feature to find out more about it.

Running 'Round the Keyboard

Most of the typing action you perform occurs on the keys located in the center of the keyboard. The next table gives you the low down on the strangely named keys that circle around the keyboard like a wagon train under attack. Proceed clockwise from the upper-left corner of the keyboard.

Key (s)	What It Does
Esc	This key gives you a quick out when you find yourself in the wrong place at the wrong time. If you pull down a menu or open a dialog box that makes you feel queasy, just press Esc to make your getaway.
F1–F12	These are the function keys. They are used alone or in conjunction with the Ctrl, Shift, or Alt key to perform various word processing tasks quickly.
Print Screen, Scroll Lock, and Pause	Once upon a time, when computer programs weren't so sophisticated, these keys actually performed useful functions. Now they just take up space so you don't have big holes in your keyboard.

(continued)

8 Running 'Round the Keyboard

Key(s)	What It Does
Insert	Normally, when you type a character, the other characters move aside to make room for the new guy. When you press Insert, the new characters eat the old characters à la Pac Man. This key also resides under the name Ins along with the zero key on the *numeric keypad* (the key arrangement with all the numbers to the right of the keyboard).
Home	Home is where the left margin is. Pressing this key moves the insertion point to the left margin. A duplicate Home key can be found on the numeric keypad.
Page Up	This key moves the insertion point up the length of your screen in the current document. You can also find PgUp sharing the 9 key on the numeric keypad — it does the same thing.
Enter	Use Enter to end a paragraph in WordPerfect or to select OK in a dialog box.
Delete	Pressing Delete eliminates characters to the right of the insertion point, as opposed to the Backspace or BkSp key, which eliminates characters to the left of the insertion point. Anything you select, from words to whole documents, can be zapped with one stroke of the Delete key. You can recognize this key as Del on the numeric keypad.
End	End moves the insertion point to the end of a line of text and is also found on the numeric keypad.
Page Down	Page Down moves the insertion point down the length of your screen in the current document. You can also find PgDn sharing the 3 key on the numeric keypad — it does the same thing.
Num Lock	If you use the keys on the numeric keypad to type a number and your insertion point starts jumping all over the place instead of typing numbers, then you don't have the Num Lock key on. Press Num Lock to make sure that the keys on the numeric keypad work as number keys and not direction keys.
←, ↑, →, and ↓	The arrow keys reside between the numeric keypad and the Ctrl key and are used to move the insertion point left, up, right, and down in the current document. They also share space on the numeric keypad with the 4, 8, 6, and 2 keys, respectively, and are the main reason that the insertion point jumps all over when you enter numbers on the numeric keypad without first pressing Num Lock.
Ctrl	Ctrl, or Control, is used with function keys and certain letter keys to make your work in WordPerfect go faster. For example, press Ctrl+N to create a new document or Ctrl+F4 to close the current document.

Mousing Around 9

Key(s)	What It Does
Alt	Alt, or Alternate, is also used with certain letters to whip WordPerfect into action. You can open pull-down menus at breakneck speed by pressing Alt and one of the hot keys (indicated by an underlined letter in each command on the menu bar). After the menu is open, you can continue to select a menu command simply by pressing the appropriate underlined letter in the menu command of choice.
Shift	Shift, for those who bypassed Typing 101 for the joys of intramural sports, is used to make lowercase (small) letters uppercase (capital) and vice versa if Caps Lock is on.
Caps Lock	If you want to REALLY GET YOUR POINT ACROSS or make your manuscript INCREDIBLY HARD FOR EDITORS TO READ AND EDIT, by all means use the Caps Lock key.

Mousing Around

The mouse is the palm-sized thing with the long thin cord (tail?) connected to your computer that you roll around (hopefully on a mouse pad next to your keyboard) to make the arrow or I-beam cursor in WordPerfect move around the screen. How well you take to using the mouse demonstrates your inherent hand-eye coordination as well as the degree to which you may have enjoyed playing video games as a youngster.

The mouse has two buttons. Though hard to believe, a time existed when you couldn't configure a mouse for a left-handed person. In those days, you just called these buttons as you saw them, that is, left and right. People would tell you to mostly left-click this and sometimes right-click that. Of course, this approach makes no sense to a left-handed person who is more comfortable using the right button most of the time. For the record, I will tell you that these buttons are alternately called the primary and secondary mouse buttons. No matter what hand you configure the mouse for, the primary mouse button is the one closest to your thumb when you grasp the mouse, and the secondary mouse button is the remaining button.

You click the primary mouse button to select things like menu items, icons, and toolbar buttons and, as I mentioned earlier, to position the insertion point in a document. Clicking the secondary mouse button sometimes opens a QuickMenu containing menu options that pertain to the part of the screen you clicked. (See the section "QuickMenus" later in this part for more information.)

10 Using Menus

The following table familiarizes you with the many methods of clicking that you can use in WordPerfect 9.

Type of Click	How To
Click	Press the primary or secondary mouse button.
Shift+click	Click the primary mouse button while holding down the Shift key.
Ctrl+click	Click the primary mouse button while holding down the Ctrl key.
Double-click	Press the primary mouse button twice, like when you impatiently tap your fingers.
Drag	Press the primary mouse button and, while still holding it down, drag (roll) the mouse. Use click and drag to select text in WordPerfect.
Drag and drop	After you drag to select text, you can click and drag the selected text again to move it to another place in your document and drop it there. To drop it, just let go of the primary mouse button. You can also use this drag-and-drop method to move file and folder icons to new locations in Windows 95 or 98.

Using Menus

This section shows you how to use the menus that contain all the commands that WordPerfect 9 performs for your word processing enjoyment.

When you open the program, you see the menu bar at the top of the screen with its eight WordPerfect pull-down menus.

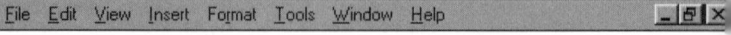

To open a pull-down menu on the menu bar, click the menu name or press Alt and the underlined letter (hot key) in the menu name. To open the File menu, for example, click File on the menu bar or press Alt+F. You are immediately confronted with a whole bunch of menu commands from which to choose.

Using Menus

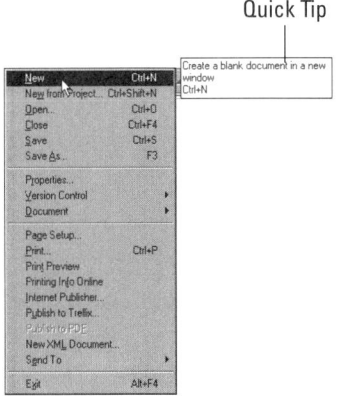

Quick Tip

To choose a command from the pull-down menu, click the command name or press the letter that is underlined in the command name. For example, to choose New at the top of the File menu, click the word New or press the letter *N* to start a new document.

The preceding figure shows WordPerfect's Quick Tip feature in action. Quick Tips are automatically enabled in a new WordPerfect document and provide concise information that speeds up the process of learning menu commands. When you roll over a menu command with the mouse pointer, a tiny box displays the function of the menu command as well as its shortcut keys when available. (See the next section to find out about shortcuts.) Once you get the hang of all the menu commands in WordPerfect and these little reminders become downright annoying, just disable Quick Tips:

1. Choose Tools⇨Settings.

2. Click Environment to open the "Environment Settings" dialog box.

3. Click the Interface tab.

4. In the "Items to display on menus" area, click to remove the check mark in the "Quick Tips" check box.

5. Click OK or press Enter.

Take the shortcut keys

WordPerfect 9 uses many of the universal shortcuts that are available in Windows 95 or 98 programs. These are key combinations that use a variety of keys (like the Ctrl key, the function keys, and various letter keys) to select a menu command via the keyboard, as

Using Menus

opposed to using the mouse to point and click the command. To save a document without going to the menu bar, for example, just press the shortcut key combination Ctrl+S.

 Many of the most often used menu commands in WordPerfect have shortcut keys. If you find yourself using the same command over and over, it probably has a shortcut key that you can use to speed up your work. WordPerfect 9 gives you the option of displaying shortcut keys next to commands on the menu bar:

1. Choose Tool⇨Settings.
2. Click Environment to open the "Environment Settings" dialog box.
3. Click the Interface tab.
4. In the "Items to display on menus" area, click to place a check mark in the "Shortcut keys" check box.
5. Click OK or press Enter.

Some of the menu commands are followed by an ellipsis (three dots). These commands open a dialog box containing the parameters that pertain to that command. See the upcoming section "Carrying On with a Dialog Box" to discover how to use these things.

QuickMenus

QuickMenus are pop-up menus that contain a bunch of commands directly related to the object to which they are attached. WordPerfect is full of useful QuickMenus. Just click around the different parts of the screen with the secondary mouse button to see whether a QuickMenu appears. You get a QuickMenu with these formatting commands when you click the secondary mouse button in the middle of a WordPerfect document:

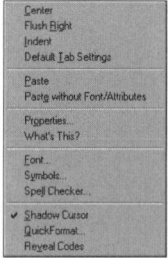

Clicking the WordPerfect 9 toolbar with the secondary mouse button brings up a QuickMenu that lets you add or delete toolbars. (See the section on toolbars in Part V.)

Carrying On with a Dialog Box

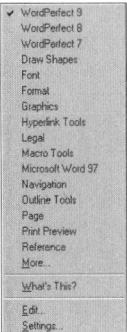

Carrying On with a Dialog Box

Some of the commands you ask WordPerfect 9 to perform require user-defined settings. Selecting one of these commands opens a dialog box where you set the parameters that the program uses to complete the task. The "Print" dialog box is a good example that shows the different controls you encounter when you ask WordPerfect to print a document.

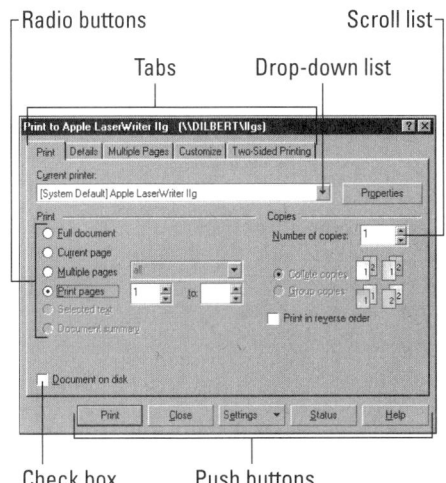

In the Print area of the "Print" dialog box, you see *radio buttons* used to select what you want to print. Keep in mind that when you encounter a set of radio buttons in a dialog box, you can select only one (just like in the radio world, where only one station can be tuned in at a time). In this example, you are given the choice of printing the full document, the current page, or a range of pages.

In the lower-left corner of the "Print" dialog box sits the "Document on disk" *check box*. Though only one check box appears in this example, a dialog box can have handfuls. Check boxes work just like radio buttons except that you can select as many as you want, or none at all, when given the option.

Next to the "Print pages" radio button are two *scroll lists* for selecting a range of pages to print. For example, if you want to print pages 2 to 4, click the up arrow on the right side of the first scroll list once and the up arrow on the second scroll list three times. Likewise, clicking the down arrows decreases the page numbers down to 1. If the document has a lot of pages, you can click in the text box and type a number — you have better things to do in life than click a scroll up button 163 times so that you can print pages 79 to 86.

In the Current printer area is a *drop-down list*. Click the down arrow on the right, and a list of printers drops down so that you can choose the right printer for the job.

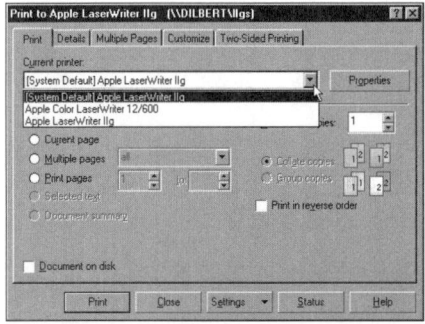

Buttons can be found anywhere, but most are located at the bottom or right side of dialog boxes. After you finish defining the settings in the "Print" dialog box, you click Print to start the job. All dialog boxes in WordPerfect 9 have a Close or Cancel button in case you change your mind about using the dialog box you opened.

The "Print" dialog box has five *tabs*. Not all dialog boxes have tabs, and some have fewer or more than this example. When you click a tab, another page of settings appears that pertains to the task at hand. Click the Details tab, and you get a page of printer details to specify.

The WordPerfect 9 Window and Its Parts

Like all good computer programs, WordPerfect 9 strives to put every imaginable feature and function right at your fingertips. As noble as this gesture is, it creates a daunting window to navigate

The WordPerfect 9 Window and Its Parts 15

for the word processor neophyte. Fortunately, WordPerfect is so user-friendly, that it's a snap to grasp how to use its features. To further you along, the following figure and table give you the rundown on the parts that make up the WordPerfect 9 window.

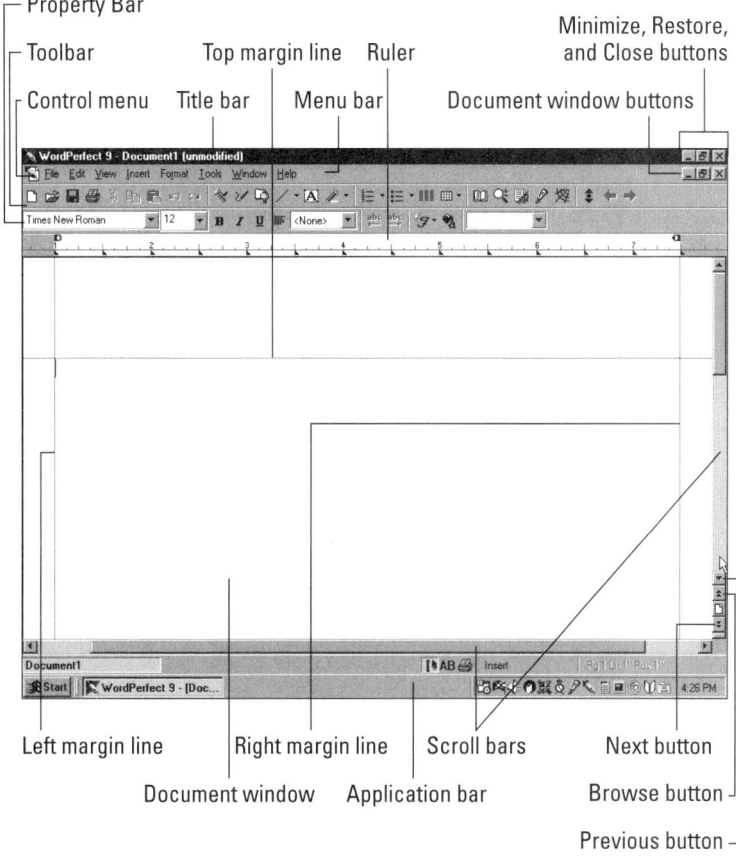

Part of the Screen	What It Is
Title bar	You find the Title bar at the very top of the screen. It contains the WordPerfect 9 icon and the name of the current document.
Control menu	If you click the Control menu button (with the WordPerfect 9 icon) just below the Title bar icon, a pull-down menu appears with a whole bunch of options for adjusting the size of the document window. You can also close the current document or go to the next open document.

(continued)

The WordPerfect 9 Window and Its Parts

Part of the Screen	What It Is
WordPerfect 9 menu bar	This bar houses the eight main menus that let you access just about all the bells and whistles that come with WordPerfect 9.
WordPerfect 9 toolbar	The WordPerfect 9 toolbar gives you a quick way to execute some of the most often used menu commands.
Property Bar	The buttons that appear on the Property Bar change when you select different components in the document. The Property Bar is context-sensitive and changes according to whether you are editing text, graphics, or tables. For example, if you select a graphic in the document, the Property Bar serves up graphic-editing buttons. By default, when you first start WordPerfect 9, the Property Bar appears basically identical to the optional Font bar. For more on this cool feature, see Part V.
Ruler	The Ruler shows you the width of your document and margins, as well as tab location. By default, WordPerfect 9 starts up with the Ruler turned off, so you may have to choose View⇨Ruler to see it.
Document window	Where all the word processing action occurs.
Left, Right, and Top margin lines	These visibly show the left, right, and top margins.
Application Bar	The Application Bar displays and lets you access information about open documents and the current state of WordPerfect 9. For more information, see Part V.
Previous, Next, and Browse buttons	These buttons, located on the vertical scroll bar, give you numerous ways to navigate your document. Use the Browse button to select whether you want to scroll through your document by page, table, box, footnote, endnote, heading, edit position, or comment; then use the Previous and Next buttons to jump to the previous or next instance of that option. See "Insertion Point" in Part II to check out new navigation features in WordPerfect 9.
Scroll bars	Scroll bars allow you to move to the far reaches of the document in a horizontal or vertical fashion.
Program window Minimize, Restore, and Close buttons	These buttons offer the quickest way to shrink, expand, and close the WordPerfect 9 program If you click the Restore button to get a mid-size window, the Restore button changes to a Maximize button, which you can click to get a full-size window.
Document window Minimize, Restore, and Close buttons	These buttons, which look the same as the buttons for the program window, do the same thing for the document window that they do for the program window. They offer the quickest way to shrink, enlarge, and close the document window.

Starting WordPerfect 9

¶ Is for Paragraph

Before I get to the final section of Part I, where you crank up WordPerfect 9 for the first time, you need to understand the significance of paragraphs as they relate to word processors.

One of the reasons that word processors are considered the greatest thing since sliced bread to many (pre-Gen-X) people is that word processors never require you to slam a carriage return or press Return when you reach the right margin. Now that's progress.

So how do you start a new paragraph when the word processor automatically types new lines merrily into the next millennium? Although you could plan all your paragraphs to end at the right margin so that you can indent the next line, the real answer is to just press Enter. (Those who actually used electric typewriters can recall when the Return key was right where the Enter key is today.) Every time you press Enter while typing, the word processor gives you a new paragraph. Whether you press Enter after a title, heading, graphic, or even a blank line doesn't matter — you get a paragraph.

Word processors clearly don't adhere to the rules of good paragraph structure when spewing out paragraphs. Word processors do put the paragraph to good use when they're formatting a document. For example, when you choose Format⇨Paragraph to apply various paragraph formatting options, the formatting changes affect the entire paragraph that contains the cursor. This approach makes formatting a paragraph really easy because you merely click in the paragraph rather than select all the text before you apply formatting.

Another advantage of this global view of paragraphs is that when you copy a paragraph symbol along with its accompanying text to another place in the document, the formatting of the copied paragraph is also copied. WordPerfect 9 gives you the option of viewing paragraph symbols in a document. Just choose View⇨Show ¶ on the menu bar to turn this feature off or on.

Starting WordPerfect 9

WordPerfect 9 gives you two easy methods of opening the program so that you can get right to work. If you like using the Windows taskbar, do this:

1. Click Start on the taskbar.

2. Choose Programs⇨WordPerfect Office 2000.

3. Choose WordPerfect 9.

18 Starting WordPerfect 9

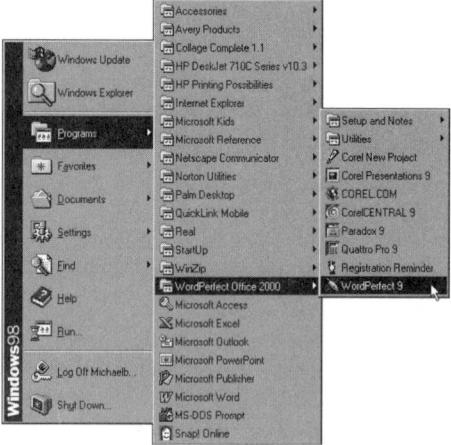

An even easier way to start WordPerfect 9 is to click the program icon on the Desktop Applications Director (DAD). The DAD Properties icon looks like four primary-colored arrows pointing inward and is located in the status area of the Windows 98 taskbar (the section on the right side of the taskbar).

The DAD automatically places program icons for the major applications in the WordPerfect 2000 suite in the status area of the Windows 95 or 98 taskbar. When you want to run one of these programs, simply click its program icon on the taskbar.

If you want to add or remove programs from the taskbar, click the DAD Properties button to open the dialog box shown in the following figure. You can also double-click any of the program icons that you currently have displayed in the "DAD Properties" dialog box to activate the "Properties" dialog box for that program.

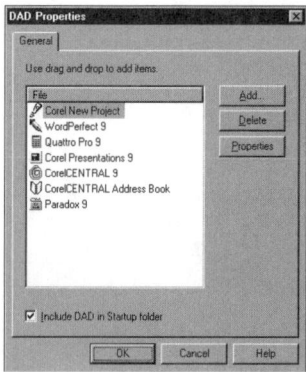

Starting WordPerfect 9

Click anywhere on DAD with the secondary mouse button to open the QuickMenu shown below. Here you can open the "DAD Properties" dialog box or select the name of any of the programs listed on the QuickMenu to launch that program.

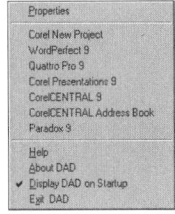

Setting Up and Editing a Document

Being a monster typist does not necessarily make you a great user of word processors (although it certainly helps). You really shine if you can set up all the bells and whistles and edit the dickens out of a document. In the process, any typing skills you possess are put to better use creating great prose (or whatever) as you let the word processor take care of all the menial tasks that, let's face it, really are beneath your nimble digits.

Part II shows you how to deal with all phases of setting up and editing a document so you can spend most of your time in WordPerfect 9 processing those words.

In this part . . .
- Selecting, deleting, cutting, copying, pasting, and generally massaging text
- Opening, closing, and saving a document
- The PerfectExpert as the perfect guest
- Lots of ways to view a page
- Writing tools
- Headers and footers

Border/Fill

This option lets you put different borders and background fills around paragraphs, pages, or columns in your document.

WordPerfect 9 makes creating borders and background fills a snap, to liven up paragraphs, pages, or columns. To use the Border/Fill feature, follow these steps:

1. Position the insertion point in the paragraph, on the page, or between the columns where you want the borders to begin.

2. Choose Format⇨Paragraph or Page and then choose Border/Fill from the submenu that appears.

If you are applying borders or fills to a column, choose Format⇨Columns and then click the "Border/Fill" button in the "Columns" dialog box.

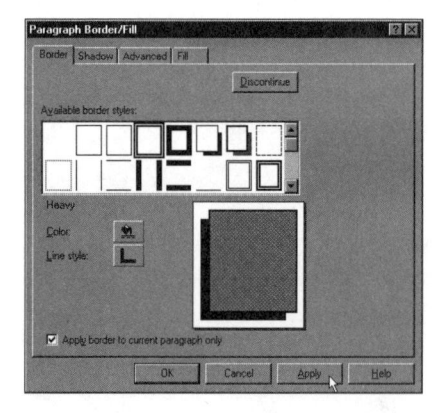

3. On the Border tab, click to select a border style in the Available border styles window.

4. Select desired options from the following tabs:

- **Shadow:** Choose a direction as well as the height, width, and color of the shadow to apply to a selected border.
- **Advanced:** Set the space inside and outside the border in relation to the text or image. Set the parameters for gradient styles applied to fills.
- **Fill:** Choose a fill style and its background and foreground color.

5. Click Apply to preview the border/fill changes in the document without closing the "Border/Fill" dialog box.

   6. Click OK or press Enter to accept the border/fill changes, close the "Border/Fill" dialog box, and return to the current document.

When you add paragraph, page, or column borders to a document, by default the "Apply border to current paragraph, page, or column only" check box is enabled. With this default, a border is applied around only the particular paragraph or group of paragraphs selected in the document.

Warning: If you remove the check mark by clicking the "Apply border to current paragraph, page, or column only" check box in the lower-left corner of the appropriate "Border/Fill" dialog box, WordPerfect 9 gets carried away and adds these borders to all subsequent paragraphs, pages, or columns in that document.

Cross-Reference: For more information about this command, see Chapter 14 of *WordPerfect 9 For Windows For Dummies*.

Cancel

This command backs you out of commands and dialog box options or discontinues a procedure before you get yourself into real trouble! Follow one of these procedures, as necessary:

- ✦ To put away a pull-down menu, click the mouse pointer somewhere in the document.
- ✦ To put away a dialog box, click Cancel. Remember that you can always rely on the Esc key to make your escape, too.

Close (Document)

This command closes the current document window and prompts you to save the file, in case you're just about to blow your work away by forgetting to save before closing. To close the current document:

   1. Click the Close button for the document window. (It's the one in the upper-right corner of the document window.)

   2. Choose File⇨Close.

Tip: When you close a document that contains information that has not been saved, the program displays a warning box that asks whether you want to save changes to your document. To save a document, click Yes or press Enter. If the document has not been saved yet, the "Save As" dialog box appears and you have to name the document. (See the "Save As" section later in this part for more information.)

Convert Case

This command changes the text you have selected to all uppercase, all lowercase, or initial capital letters.

To convert the case of specific text:

1. Select the text. See the section "Select (Text)" later in this part for details.

2. Choose Edit⇨Convert Case.

3. Choose from the following options:

- lowercase to convert all the letters to lowercase
- UPPERCASE to convert them all to uppercase
- Initial Capitals to capitalize only the first letter of each word

Cut, Copy, and Paste

These commands enable you to move or copy blocks of text within the same document or to different documents that are open in other document windows.

Do you wanna move or copy?

When you move text in a document, you literally cut it out and take it somewhere else, as opposed to copying, which leaves an identical remnant behind. The procedures, no matter which option you choose, go like this:

1. Select the text. See the section "Select (Text)" later in this part for details.

2. Press Ctrl+X to cut or Ctrl+C to copy the text.

3. Click to place the insertion point at the text's final destination.

4. Press Ctrl+V to paste the text at the new insertion point.

Although you can perform the cut, copy, and paste commands from the Edit menu, it is the most tedious way to accomplish these basic tasks.

A few caveats

The Cut, Copy, and Paste commands use a special area of memory, called the Clipboard, that temporarily holds the information to be moved or copied.

When you use Cut, Copy, and Paste, keep in mind that the Clipboard normally holds only one block of selected text at a time. Any new text you copy or cut to the Clipboard completely replaces the text that is already there. The only way to add information to the Clipboard is to use the Append command on the Edit menu. The selected text you place in the Clipboard stays there until you replace it (by using Cut or Copy); you can use the Paste command, however, to copy the selected text over and over again in any document.

The issue of which set of Cut, Copy, and Paste procedures is faster is up in the air, but I'll give you the toolbar method so you can get out your stop watches and compare it with the shortcut key method. These buttons reside on the WordPerfect 9 toolbar:

+ **Cut button:** Cut the selected text to the Clipboard.
+ **Copy button:** Copy the selected text to the Clipboard.
+ **Paste button:** Paste the contents of the Clipboard at the insertion point's current position.

To use these buttons, follow along:

1. Select the text. See the section "Select (Text)" later in this part for details.

2. Click the Cut button to cut or the Copy button to copy the text.

3. Click to place the insertion point at the text's final destination.

4. Click the Paste button to paste the text at the new insertion point.

Keep in mind that you don't have to go through all the cut- or copy-and-paste rigmarole — you can also move or copy text with the good old drag-and-drop method. See the section "Drag and Drop (Text)" later in this part for details.

Delete (Text)

WordPerfect 9 provides loads of ways to get rid of text.

The easiest way to delete text is as follows:

1. Select the text. See the section "Select (Text)" later in this part for details.

2. Press Delete or Backspace.

You can use any of the keystrokes in the following table to delete text using the keyboard.

Keystroke	What It Deletes
Backspace	Character to the left of the insertion point
Delete	The character or space to the right of the insertion point
Ctrl+Backspace	The word to the left of the insertion point, including the space after the word
Ctrl+Delete	From the insertion point to the end of the current line

Don't forget the Undo command (press Ctrl+Z) for those times when you make a boo-boo and blow away text you shouldn't have.

For more information about this command, see the section "Undo" later in this part.

Document Information

(See "Properties" later in this part.)

Document Summary

(See "Properties" later in this part.)

Draft View

This feature displays your document without the top and bottom margins and without such special stuff as headers, footers, page numbers, or footnotes that show up in the top and bottom margins.

To change the current page view to Draft view, choose View⇨Draft or press Ctrl+F5.

Draft view does not display watermarks you may be using. Because not all features display, working in Draft view is often faster than working in Page view.

Switch to Draft view when you want to get the maximum amount of text on-screen for editing. Switch to Page view when you want to see the relationship between the body text and the top and bottom margins or when you want to see special elements, such as headers and footers, on-screen.

See also the sections "Page View," "Two Page View," and "Zoom" in this part.

Drag and Drop (Text)

This feature allows you mouse maniacs to move or copy selected text to a new place in the document. Just drag the selection to its new position and then drop it in place by releasing the mouse button.

To move text with the drag-and-drop feature:

1. Select the text you want to move. See the section "Select (Text)" later in this part for details.

2. Position the mouse pointer somewhere within the selection and hold down the mouse button.

3. Drag the mouse pointer to the new place in the document where you want the block to appear.

   As you drag the mouse pointer, a small rectangle appears, which indicates that the drag-and-drop process is happening.

4. Release the mouse button to insert the block of text in its new position in the document.

TIP: To copy selected text rather than move it, follow the same procedure just described, but press and hold Ctrl as you drag the selected block of text.

TIP: You can select the current word by double-clicking it; the sentence by triple-clicking it; and the paragraph by quadruple-clicking it.

Exit WordPerfect

This command quits WordPerfect 9 and returns you to the Windows desktop or any other open program.

TIP: When you choose File⇔Exit from the menu bar and have documents open that contain edits you have not saved, a message dialog box appears for each unsaved document and asks whether you want to save the changes. To save the document, click Yes. To abandon the changes, click No (first be sure that you really, really don't want the information).

Find and Replace

This tool lets you quickly locate certain text or secret codes in a document. If you use the Replace command, you can have WordPerfect 9 replace the search text with other text on a case-by-case basis or globally throughout the entire document.

28 Find and Replace

Here's how to find and replace text or codes:

1. Press Ctrl+F to open the "Find and Replace" dialog box.

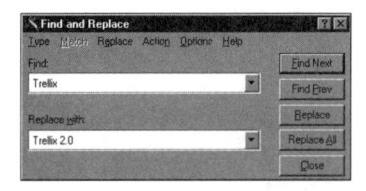

2. Type the search text in the "Find" text box.

3. Type the replace text in the "Replace with" text box.

4. Select from the following menu options:

- **Type:** Lets you choose between searching and replacing Text (the default), Word Forms, or Specific Codes.

- **Match:** Lets you search for whole words only, specify an exact case match, search for text in a particular font or attribute, or search for secret codes.

- **Replace:** Lets you replace text without regard to format or text in a particular font or attribute, or to replace certain secret codes.

- **Action:** Lets you specify which type of action WordPerfect should take when it finds the search text in your document. The actions include selecting the matched text and placing the insertion point before or after the matched text. You can even extend the selection from the search starting point right through matched text.

- **Options:** Among other things, you can choose how, where, and what kinds of text to search for.

5. After you've thoroughly defined the search parameters, click one of these buttons:

- **Find Next:** Finds the next occurrence of the text, searching forward from the insertion point.

- **Find Prev:** Finds the first previous occurrence of the search text, searching backward from the insertion point.

- **Replace:** Selects the text the first time it is found and then replaces the text each time you click Replace.

- **Replace All:** Finds and replaces each occurrence of the text or codes.

Footnotes and Endnotes

6. After your search is over, click <u>C</u>lose to shut down the "Find and Replace" dialog box and return to the current document.

After the search is on, you can use these shortcut keys to speed up the process:

✦ **Press Alt+F:** to find the next occurrence of the search text.

✦ **Press Alt+P:** to find the previous occurrence of the search text.

If you ever mess up and replace a bunch of text or secret codes with the wrong stuff, immediately close the "Find and Replace" dialog box before you do anything else to the document. Then choose <u>E</u>dit⇨<u>U</u>ndo or press Ctrl+Z to put the text back to the way it was.

Footnotes and Endnotes

This tool lets you add footnotes, which appear throughout the text at the bottom of every page, or endnotes, which are grouped together at the end of the document. WordPerfect 9 automatically numbers both types of notes so that you don't have to drive yourself crazy renumbering the darn things by hand when you have to add a note or take one out.

Creating a footnote or endnote

To create a footnote or an endnote in the text of your document, follow these steps:

1. Position the insertion point in the text where you want the footnote or endnote reference number to appear.

2. Choose <u>I</u>nsert⇨<u>F</u>ootnote/Endnote to open the "Footnote/Endnote" dialog box.

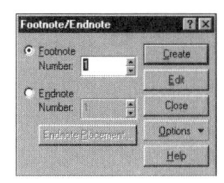

3. Select the "<u>F</u>ootnote" or "E<u>n</u>dnote" radio button.

Footnotes and Endnotes

4. Click Create.

WordPerfect 9 inserts the number of the footnote or endnote in the document and positions the insertion point at the bottom of the page (for footnotes) or the end of the document (for endnotes). At the same time, WordPerfect 9 displays the Footnote/Endnote icons in the Property bar.

5. Type the text of the footnote or endnote and then click the Close button on the Footnote/Endnote Property Bar.

Editing text in a footnote or endnote

1. Choose Insert⇔Footnote/Endnote.

2. Select the "Footnote Number" or the "Endnote Number" radio button.

3. Use the scroll list to enter the number of the footnote or endnote to which you want to make changes.

4. Click the Edit button to close the "Footnote/Endnote" dialog box and position the insertion point at the beginning of the note text so that you can make your editing changes.

> **TIP:** If you're in Page view (see the "Page View" section later in this part for details), you can edit the text of a footnote directly at the bottom of the page by clicking the insertion point wherever you want the edits and then beginning to edit.

> **TIP:** When you're entering the text for your note, you can use the WordPerfect 9 toolbar and Property bar to select the editing and formatting commands you need in order to edit the text, including the Spell Checker and Thesaurus.

Changing the footnote or endnote numbering

WordPerfect 9 automatically numbers your footnotes and endnotes and starts with the number 1. You can restart the numbering of your footnotes or endnotes at a particular place in the document (at a section break, for example). Here's how to perform this nifty feat:

1. Position the insertion point in front of the footnote or endnote number in the text to be renumbered.

2. Choose Insert⇔Footnote/Endnote to open the "Footnote/Endnote" dialog box.

3. Choose Options⇔Set Number to open the "Footnote Number" or "Endnote Number" dialog box.

Header/Footer **31**

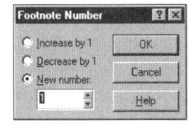

4. Choose from these options:

- **Increase by 1:** Click to increase the note number by one.
- **Decrease by 1:** Click to decrease the note number by one.
- **New Number:** Click to enter a nonconsecutive number.

5. Click OK and then Close to close the "Footnote/Endnote" dialog box and return to the current document.

> **TIP**
> To renumber all the footnotes or endnotes in your document, move the insertion point to the beginning of the document.

Grammatik

(See "Writing Tools" later in this part.)

Header/Footer

This tool adds to the document a header, which prints the same information at the top of each page, or a footer, which prints the same information at the bottom of each page.

WordPerfect 9 lets you create two different headers and two different footers within a document. You can have one header on all even pages and another on all odd pages, for example. To create a header or footer for the document, follow these steps:

1. Position the insertion point somewhere on the first page of the document where you want the header or footer to appear.

If you want the header or footer to appear on every page of the document, make sure that your insertion point is on page one. If you don't want the header or footer to appear on the first page, make sure that your insertion point is on page two (or whichever page the header or footer appears on first).

2. Choose Insert⇨Header/Footer.

This step opens the "Headers/Footers" dialog box.

Header/Footer

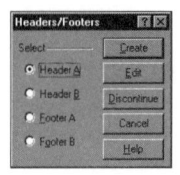

3. Choose from the following options:

   - **Header A:** Click to create a header.
   - **Header B:** Click to create a second header.
   - **Footer A:** Click to create a footer.
   - **Footer B:** Click to create a second footer.

4. Click Create to position the insertion point at the top or bottom of the page, depending on whether you chose a header or a footer.

   This step also displays the Header/Footer Property Bar.

5. Type the text for your header or footer.

   You can format the header or footer text with these formatting commands on the Header/Footer Property Bar:

   - **Number:** To add a page number to your header or footer.
   - **Horizontal Line:** To add a graphics line to the header or footer.
   - **Header/Footer Placement:** To make the header or footer appear only on even- or odd-numbered pages.
   - **Header/Footer Distance:** To increase or decrease the spacing between the header or footer and the body of the document.

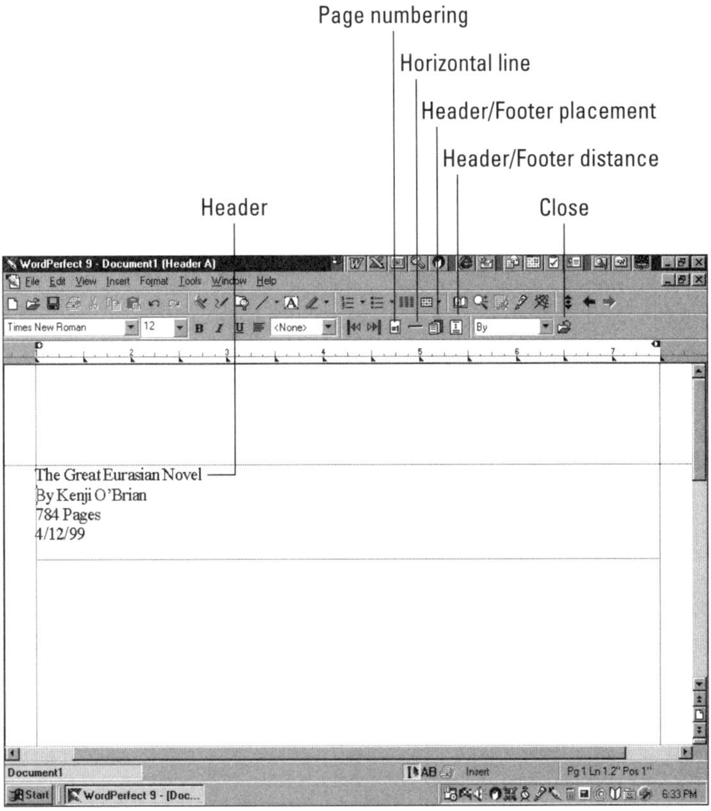
Page numbering
Horizontal line
Header/Footer placement
Header/Footer distance
Header
Close
WordPerfect 9 - Document1 (Header A)
The Great Eurasian Novel
By Kenji O'Brian
784 Pages
4/12/99

6. After you finish entering and formatting the header or footer text, click Close on the Header/Footer Property Bar to hide the Header/Footer icons on the Property bar and to return to the normal document window.

TIP

WordPerfect 9 also lets you create a watermark, which is sort of like a header or footer. It prints very lightly in the background so that the text in your document can still be read. See Part VI for details.

Help

This feature provides help in using a particular WordPerfect 9 feature when you're valiantly trying to figure out how to get the program to do what you want.

34 Help

Apparently, the entire WordPerfect 9 owner manual is packed into the program itself. Although the resource is comprehensive, to put it mildly, it is also easy to access. To enter into the vast world of online help, follow these steps:

1. Press F1 or choose Help⇨Help Topics to open the "Help Topics: WordPerfect 9 Help" dialog box.

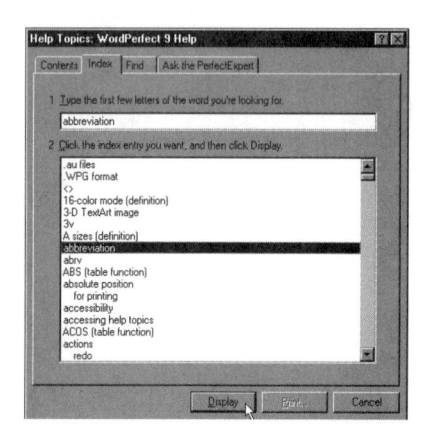

2. Click to select one of the following tabs:

- **Contents:** Displays Help topics organized by category. Double-click a book icon to see which topics are in that category. Double-click a topic to check it out.

- **Index:** Displays the Help Index. Type a topic you want to find, or scroll through the list of index entries. After you find an entry that appeals to you, click to select it, and then click Display.

- **Find:** A tedious search engine that you'll probably rarely use.

- **Ask the PerfectExpert:** You can ask the PerfectExpert questions in your own words (or another's if you need that kind of help, too) and even let the PerfectExpert guide you through a word-processing project. See the "PerfectExpert" section later in this part for more on this cool feature.

3. When you find a topic you want to digest, click Display to view it on-screen.

4. After you have all the help you need, click the Close button to return to the open document.

You can also get help using a particular menu command or dialog box option as you're trying to use the darn things. To use context-sensitive help, do the following:

Hyphenation 35

[?] **1.** Click the What's This? icon on the upper-right corner of a dialog box.

2. Place the pointer on the item you want information about and click.

A QuickTip appears on-screen, giving you the lowdown on the item you've selected.

(Fast Track) You can display an available menu command or dialog box QuickTip by clicking on the item in question with the secondary mouse button.

Hyphenation

This feature automatically hyphenates words in a paragraph to reduce the raggedness of the right margin (when you're using left justification) or the white space between words in the lines (when you're using full justification).

To have WordPerfect 9 automatically hyphenate the words in your document according to the program's dictionary, follow these steps:

1. Position the insertion point at the place in the document where you want to turn hyphenation on. Or to hyphenate the entire document, press Ctrl+Home, which moves the insertion point to the beginning of the document.

2. Choose Tools⇨Language⇨Hyphenation to open the "Line Hyphenation" dialog box.

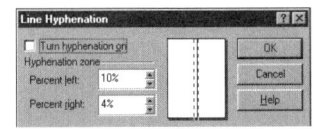

```
Line Hyphenation                          [?][X]
☐ Turn hyphenation on
Hyphenation zone                          [ OK ]
  Percent left:  10%                      [Cancel]
  Percent right: 4%                       [ Help ]
```

3. Click the "Turn hyphenation on" check box to put a check mark in it.

For future reference, you remove the check mark from this check box to turn hyphenation off.

4. Click OK or press Enter.

As you add text from the insertion point's position or scroll through the document, WordPerfect 9 displays the "Position Hyphen" dialog box. This box prompts you to confirm its suggested hyphenation of the word (if that word isn't in the spelling dictionary).

Hyphenation

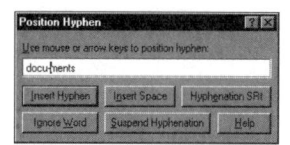

Here's a closer look at the options in the "Position Hyphen" dialog box:

- ✦ **Use mouse or arrow keys to position hyphen:** Repositions the hyphen in the word that appears in the text box.

- ✦ **Insert Hyphen:** Accepts the position of the hyphen as it is displayed.

- ✦ **Insert Space:** Inserts a space rather than a hyphen.

- ✦ **Hyphenation SRt:** Inserts a hyphenation soft return to break the word without inserting a space.

- ✦ **Ignore Word:** Wraps the entire word to the next line rather than break the word with a hyphen.

- ✦ **Suspend Hyphenation:** Temporarily suspends the hyphenation (so that you can do something else, such as scroll the text or check its spelling).

WordPerfect 9 maintains a hot zone, made up of the left and right hyphenation zones, that determines when a word is up for hyphenation. To be a candidate for hyphenation, a word must begin within the left zone and then extend beyond the right zone.

You have two ways to change how often WordPerfect 9 bugs you to hyphenate words:

- ✦ You can monkey around with the size of the left and right zones. To do so, open the "Line Hyphenation" dialog box and change the percentages in the "Percent left" and "Percent right" text boxes.

    Increasing the zone percentages hyphenates fewer words, and decreasing the percentages hyphenates more words.

- ✦ You can define how and when WordPerfect 9 displays the "Position Hyphen" dialog box in the Prompts tab of the "Environment Settings" dialog box. Choose Tools⇨Settings, click the Environment icon on the Settings panel, and click the Prompts tab. In the Prompt area, choose When Required, Always, or Never on the "On hyphenation:" drop-down list box.

For more information about hyphenation, see Chapter 8 of *WordPerfect 9 For Windows For Dummies*.

Insertion Point

Before you edit the text of your document, you have to position the insertion point in the correct place. WordPerfect 9 restricts insertion-point movement to the existing text in a document and never lets you move it beyond the last character in a document.

WordPerfect 9 offers a variety of ways to move the insertion point with the keyboard, as shown in the following table.

Keystrokes	Where Insertion Point Moves
←	Next character or space to the left
→	Next character or space to the right
Ctrl+←	Beginning of the next word to the left
Ctrl+→	Beginning of the next word to the right
Ctrl+↑	Beginning of the current or preceding paragraph
Ctrl+↓	Beginning of the next paragraph
Home	Left edge of the current screen or beginning of the current line
End	Right edge of the current screen or end of the current line
Ctrl+Home	Beginning of the document
Ctrl+End	End of the document
PgUp	Up a screen
PgDn	Down a screen
Alt+PgUp	Top of the current page
Alt+PgDn	Top of the next page

If you use the mouse, you can reposition the insertion point in the document text by placing the mouse pointer on the character or space and clicking the primary mouse button. See "Shadow Cursor" in Part V to learn how to quickly place the insertion point anywhere in your document.

WARNING

Don't confuse the insertion point with the mouse pointer (as easy as that mistake is to make). The insertion point keeps your place in the document as it continues to blink. The mouse pointer enables you to select things (as well as reposition the insertion point in the text). Mostly, the mouse pointer just lies there on-screen, not doing anything useful and getting in the way until you move the mouse.

Line Spacing

The tasks in this section deal with changing the line spacing of the text in your document.

To change line spacing:

1. Position the insertion point on the first line to be affected.

2. Choose Format⇨Line⇨Spacing to open the "Line Spacing" dialog box.

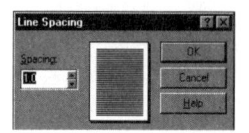

3. Enter the new spacing in the Spacing text box (or select the new spacing using the scroll list buttons). The controls let you select by tenths, where 1.0 equals single-spaced and 2.0 equals double-spaced text.

4. Click OK or press Enter.

When you set the line spacing for your document, WordPerfect 9 lets you enter values in increments that are smaller than one-half a line. Keep in mind, however, that your printer may not be able to handle anything smaller than a half line. Whenever possible, WordPerfect 9 displays the new line spacing on-screen more or less as it prints.

For more information about this command, see Chapter 8 of *WordPerfect 9 For Windows For Dummies*.

New (Document)

You have to start somewhere, and WordPerfect 9 makes it easy to begin a new document.

Opening a new document

Here are the three WFR (Windows from Redmond) approved methods of opening a new document in WordPerfect 9.

✦ Press Ctrl+N.

✦ Click New on the WordPerfect 9 toolbar.

✦ Choose File⇨New.

New (Document) 39

TIP

Unless you started WordPerfect 9 by opening a previously saved document (see "Open (Document)" in just a bit), the program always opens with a blank document generically titled Document1. In fact, even when you close all documents in WordPerfect 9, a new blank document automatically appears. The preceding three commands give you a new generically titled document (Document2, and so on) in addition to the default new document. Because the program is so relentless about giving you a new document, the only reason to use these commands is if you want to create a number of new documents to work on at the same time.

Selecting a template for the new document

You can select a WordPerfect 9 template that you want to associate with your new document.

WordPerfect 9 comes with a whole bunch of premade templates that you can use for different types of documents. Each template includes the format settings, menu arrangements, toolbars, and macros required for creating a certain type of document (such as memoranda or legal briefs).

To select a new template, follow these steps:

1. Choose File⇨New from Project or press Ctrl+Shift+N to open the "Perfect Expert" dialog box.

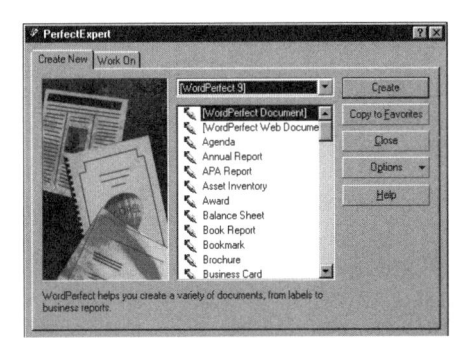

2. Select the type of document that you're about to create from the drop-down list in the upper-right corner of the dialog box.

3. Select the name of the particular template you want to use in the scroll list below the category drop-down list.

4. Click C_r_eate or press Enter to open a new document using the template you just selected.

In some cases, WordPerfect 9 opens a "Template Information" dialog box, where you can enter personal information unique to the document you're creating. Fill in any information desired or none at all.

5. Click OK or press Enter to start filling in the necessary information in the template.

When you open a template, the PerfectExpert also appears, to guide you through the process. More on the PerfectExpert later in this part.

6. After you finish filling in the different fields of the template, click OK or press Enter to open a new document using the layout of the selected template and containing the information you entered in these fields.

In addition to using the premade templates that come with WordPerfect 9, if you're adventurous enough, you can create custom templates of your own.

Open (Document)

This command opens the file you specify into a brand-new document window.

The magic of opening a document you created in another time space is performed like this:

1. Choose File⇨Open or press Ctrl+O to open the "Open File" dialog box.

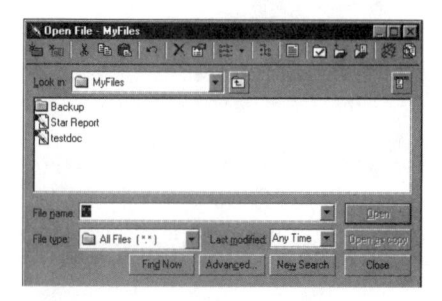

2. Use these different parts of the "Open File" dialog box to find the document you want to open:

- **Look in:** Use the "Look in" drop-down list to select the drive or folder that contains the document. Click the Up One Level button to move up through the file hierarchy.
- **File type:** Choose the type of file that appears in the "Open File" dialog box window.
- **File name:** Type the name of the document you want to open.
- **Find Now:** QuickFinder is now directly available through the "Open" dialog box. Use Find to look in the QuickFinder Search Results folder to find files that meet the criteria you specify. For example, you can search for a file type (such as *.wpd) or the file content. See the "QuickFinder" section in Part V for more details.

3. After you find the file you want to open, double-click the file icon or click Open to open it, or open a *copy* of the file by clicking Open as copy.

TIP: If you try to open a file not created with WordPerfect 9, the program opens the "Convert File Format" dialog box:

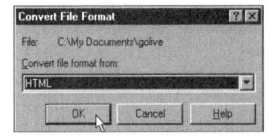

The correct file format is most likely listed in the Convert file format from text box. If the correct format is highlighted, click OK or press Enter. Otherwise, choose the correct file format in the drop-down list box and click OK or press Enter.

Page Borders

(See "Border/Fill" earlier in this part.)

Page Break

This tool inserts a hard (or manual) page break at the insertion point's position. Use this command whenever you want to place text on a completely new page:

1. Click to place the insertion point where you want to begin the new page.

2. Choose Insert⇨New Page or press Ctrl+Enter.

TIP: Don't insert hard page breaks until after you have made all your editing changes in the document. Otherwise, when you print the document, you can easily end up with blank pages or pages that have just a little bit of text. Also, remember that WordPerfect 9 provides a number of commands to keep certain text together on a page no matter how you edit the text. You don't have to use hard page breaks to keep text from being separated if you use these commands (see the section "Keep Text Together" in Part VI).

Page Numbering

This tool adds page numbers to your document, which WordPerfect 9 automatically keeps up-to-date as you edit.

To add this long form helper to your document, follow these steps:

1. Place the insertion point in the page you want to begin numbering (page one if the whole document needs page numbers).

2. Choose Format⇨Page⇨Numbering to open the "Select Page Numbering Format" dialog box:

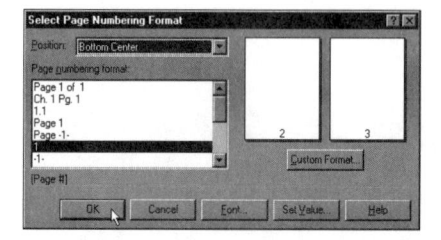

3. Choose from the following options:

   • **Position:** Choose the position of the page numbers from the drop-down list (which is then reflected in the sample pages on the right side of the dialog box).

- **Page Numbering Format:** From the scroll list, choose among many numbering formats that include not only numbers and text but also letters and Roman numerals.
- **Custom Format:** Choose or create new custom numbering codes in the "Custom Page Numbering" dialog box.
- **Font:** Choose a new font, font style, font size, text color, shading, and appearance for the page numbers in the "Page Numbering Font" dialog box.
- **Set Value:** Change the initial page number for page.

4. After you've considered all the options, click OK or press Enter to see the page numbering results in the current document.

Rather than use the Page Numbering command to number the pages in your document, you can create a header or footer that displays the page number (see the section "Header/Footer" earlier in this part).

For more information about this command, see Chapter 9 of *WordPerfect 9 For Windows For Dummies*.

Page View

This feature displays your entire document, including margins, headers, footers, page numbers, and footnotes (this view is the default in WordPerfect 9).

To switch to Page view, choose View➪Page or press Alt+F5.

Switch to Draft view when you want to maximize the amount of text on-screen and don't want to see stuff that's placed in the top and bottom margins.

For more information, refer to the sections "Draft View" earlier in this part; "Two Page View" and "Zoom," both later in this part; and "Web Page View" in Part VII.

Paragraph Borders

(See "Border/Fill" earlier in this part.)

PerfectExpert

WordPerfect 9 comes with its own built-in expert ready to help you with any task. The PerfectExpert gives you quick access to all the tools needed to create or edit a project from start to finish. To awaken the PerfectExpert:

1. Choose Help➪PerfectExpert or click the PerfectExpert button on the WordPerfect 9 toolbar.

The "Corel PerfectExpert" dialog box plants itself on the left side of the document window, begging you to test its expertise.

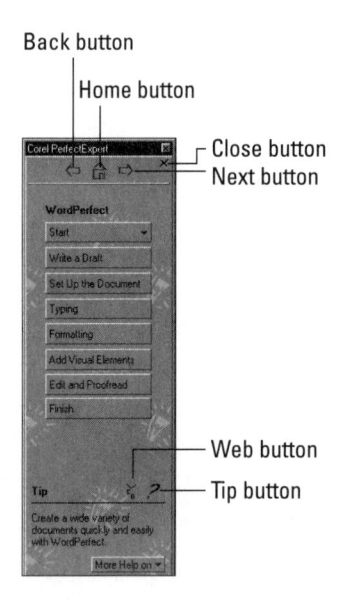

Back button
Home button
Close button
Next button
Web button
Tip button

2. Use these features to tap into the PerfectExpert's power:

- **Start:** Open a new or existing document or start a new project.
- **Write a Draft:** Focus on a subject and create an outline.
- **Set Up the Document:** Change formatting elements like margins, page size, and initial font.
- **Typing:** Insert tabs, indents, headings, and other elements.
- **Formatting:** Add columns, tables, and other elements.
- **Add Visual Elements:** Add clip art, lines, shapes, and so on.

- **Edit and Proofread:** Collaborate with someone else and check the document.
- **Finish:** Save, print, publish, and send the document.
- **Tip:** Opens the Ask the "PerfectExpert" dialog box, where you can type a question and find a solution.

3. Click a button to get help at the appropriate stage of your project.

When you click these buttons, the PerfectExpert displays a new button palette with specific commands related to the category you've chosen. This figure shows the button palette that appears after you click Set Up the Document:

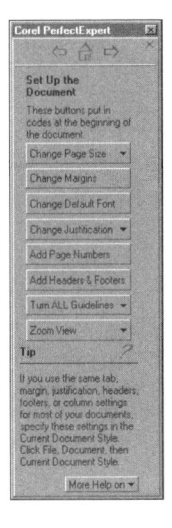

Clicking any of the buttons shown in this figure takes you to a specific dialog box. You can return to the PerfectExpert set up screen at any time by clicking Home and then exit by clicking Close.

> The PerfectExpert represents but a small part of the online help system built into WordPerfect 9. For much more on the help options at your disposal, see the "Help" section earlier in this part.

Properties

The Properties command lets you create a document summary and get statistics on a document.

46 Properties

Choose File➪Properties to open the "Properties" dialog box. The "Properties" dialog box contains the following tabs:

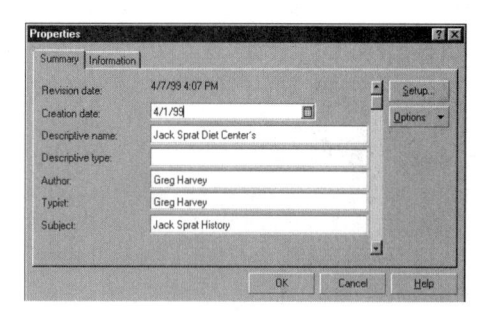

+ **Summary:** Lets you add lots of different kinds of information about the document, including such stuff as a descriptive filename (rather than that cryptic DOS monstrosity) and file type (such as memo or report), the author's and typist's names, and the document subject.

The summary tab contains the following fields for entering document information (use the scroll bar to view all the fields):

- **Descriptive name:** Lets you enter a long name for a file.

- **Descriptive type:** Lets you enter a classification or category for a document, such as legal brief or contract.

- **Creation date:** Indicates the date the document was created. WordPerfect 9 automatically enters in this text box the date you create the document summary. If the date that is entered is not the date you created the document, click the Calendar button to the right of this text box and choose the correct date in the pop-up calendar.

- **Revision date:** Indicates the date the document was last revised. WordPerfect 9 automatically updates the document summary by entering the date you last opened, edited, and saved the document (which you cannot change), in this text box.

- **Author:** Identifies the document's author.

- **Typist:** Identifies the document's typist.

- **Subject:** Identifies the subject of the document.

- **Account:** Identifies the account number for the document.

- **Keywords:** Lets you add terms you can search for later by enabling QuickFinder in the "Open File" dialog box.

Save

- **Abstract:** Lets you add a brief synopsis of the document's contents.

- **Setup:** Lets you choose which fields are included in the document summary.

- **Options:** Lets you print or delete the summary, extract information according to particular fields of the summary, or save the summary in a separate file.

✦ **Information:** Gives you oodles of statistics about your document, such as the number of characters, words, lines, sentences, and paragraphs it contains, as well as the average word length and number of words per sentence.

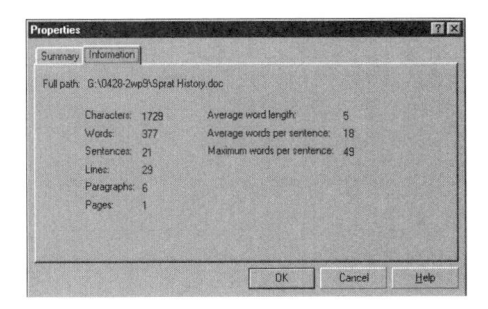

> **TIP:** You can edit a document summary from anywhere in the document by choosing File⇨Properties. You can use the enable QuickFinder option in the "Open and Save File" dialog box to locate documents quickly by searching their summary information.

Save

Lets you save your changes to a document on disk so that you have a copy of the document for future use. The first time you save, you must give the document a new filename.

Saving a file for the first time

To save a file for the first time, you have to go through the whole rigmarole described in this section:

1. Choose File⇨Save or press Ctrl+S.

The program displays the "Save File" dialog box.

Save

2. Use the "Save in" drop-down list box and the Up One Level button to locate the folder in which you want the file to be saved (unless you want them all saved in the WordPerfect default folder called MyFiles).

   The various folders appear in the "Save File" dialog box window.

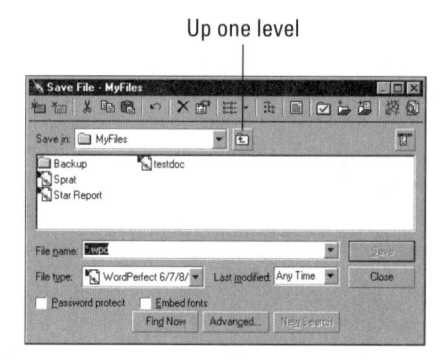

3. Type the name for your new file in the File name text box.

4. To assign a password to your file, choose the Password protect option by putting a check mark in its check box.

5. Click Save or press Enter to save the document.

   If you checked the "Password protect" check box, the "Password Protection" dialog box appears:

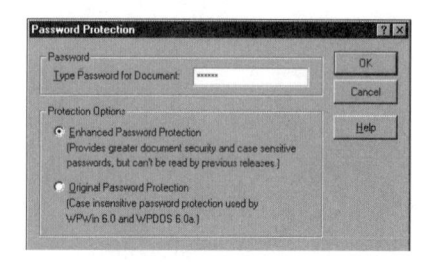

6. In the Type Password for Document text box, type the password just as you want, though you can't see it because WordPerfect 9 masks each character you type with asterisks.

   You can choose between two different degrees of password security using the "Enhanced Password Protection" or "Original Password Protection" radio button.

Save As

7. Click OK or press Enter.

8. Retype the password exactly as you originally typed it and again click OK or press Enter.

If you mess up and type the password a little differently the second time, WordPerfect 9 lets you know that the passwords don't match and you can try again.

Embedded fonts

The new WordPerfect 9 embedded font feature ensures that the fonts you select for your document are displayed whether or not those fonts are installed on the viewer's computer. When saving your document, click to place a check mark in the "Embed fonts" check box of the "Save" dialog box. WordPerfect compresses the font information along with the file data. Now your favorite fonts will go wherever your file goes for the presentation that you expect.

Spare yourself lots of heartbreak and wasted time by saving your documents often. Save every time you are interrupted (by the telephone, your boss, or whatever) and save whenever you have made more changes to the document than you would ever want to have to redo.

Saving a file on subsequent occasions

After you've saved a document for the first time, you can use these methods to save your changes to that file as you continue to work:

+ Choose File⇨Save.

+ Press Ctrl+S.

+ Click the Save button on the WordPerfect 9 toolbar.

Save As

This command lets you change the name or location of your WordPerfect 9 document. You can even save your document in a different file format. This way, coworkers less fortunate than you who have to use some other word processor can have access to your document.

As you may expect, the Save As feature is remarkably similar to the Save feature, as you will see:

50 Save As

1. Choose File⇨Save As to open the "Save As" dialog box.

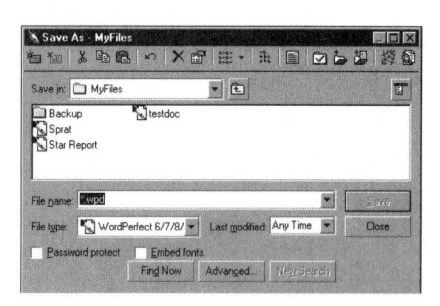

2. Use the following options in the "Save As" dialog box:

- **Save in:** Use the drop-down list to select the drive or folder that will contain the document. Click the Up One Level button to move up through the file hierarchy.

- **File name:** Type the new name of the document you want to save. You do not have to type the dot and the three letter file extension because Word Perfect adds them automatically.

- **File type:** Choose the type of file you want to save as. (Normally, you choose the default in WordPerfect versions 6, 7, and 8.)

- **Find Now:** QuickFinder is now directly available through the "Save File" and "Save As" dialog boxes. Use Find to look in the QuickFinder Search Results folder to find files that meet the criteria you specify. For example, you can search for a file type (such as *.wpd) or the file content. See the "QuickFinder" section in Part V for more details.

- **Password protect:** Password-protect your file if you like. Writing down all passwords and storing them in a secure place is a good idea. This way, coworkers can get into your files if you suddenly decide to chuck it all and live in Tahiti.

- **Last modified:** Use this drop-down list to find a proper folder to save your file to if you want to categorize your file by a specific or approximate date.

> **TIP**
> Choose File⇨Save when you want to save editing and formatting changes to the document and update the file. Use Save As to save the document with a new filename or in a new directory, in another file format for use with another word processor, or if someone convinces you that you need to add a password to the document.

Select (Text)

This tool marks a section of text so that you can do all sorts of neat things to it, such as cut and paste it, spell-check it, print it, or even get rid of it.

Natural selection

Please follow along to discover the myriad ways of selecting text:

- ✦ Position the mouse pointer in front of the first character of text that is to be highlighted and drag the pointer through the entire block of text you want to select.

- ✦ To select the current word, double-click somewhere in the word.

- ✦ To select the current sentence, triple-click somewhere in the paragraph.

- ✦ To select a block of text, click the insertion point in front of the first character, press and hold Shift, and then click the last character.

The QuickMenu method

You can also use the ubiquitous QuickMenu to select text:

1. Click the secondary mouse button in the margin to the left of the text you want to select.

2. In the menu that appears, choose one of the following:

   - **Select Sentence:** To select the current sentence.
   - **Select Paragraph:** To select the current paragraph.
   - **Select Page:** To select the current page.
   - **Select All:** To select the entire document.

> **TIP:** You don't need to select a word to apply formatting. Click anywhere in the word, and then make the change.

Other slick ways to extend a block

WordPerfect 9 offers all sorts of fast ways to extend a block of text after you've selected it. This list shows a few shortcuts you may want to try:

- ✦ **Ctrl+Shift+→:** Extend the block to the next word to the right.

- ✦ **Ctrl+Shift+←:** Extend the block to the next word to the left.

- **Ctrl+Shift+↑:** Extend the block up one line.
- **Ctrl+Shift+↓:** Extend the block down one line.
- **Ctrl+Shift+Home:** Extend the selection from the insertion point to the beginning of the document.
- **Ctrl+Shift+End:** Extend the selection from the insertion point to the end of the document.

TIP: If you ever find yourself selecting the wrong text, you can cancel the selection by pressing F8 or by clicking the insertion point anywhere in the document.

Show ¶

This command displays symbols on the screen for each code you have entered in your document, including hard return, space, tab, indent, centering, flush right, soft hyphen, center page, and advance.

Choose View⇨Show ¶ or press Ctrl+Shift+F3 to turn this feature off and on.

TIP: You can define which codes are to be represented by symbols on the screen by following these steps:

1. Choose Tools⇨Settings to open the "Settings" dialog box.

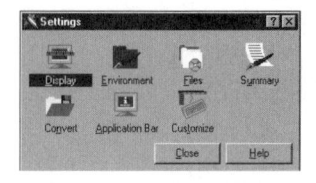

2. Click the Display button.

The "Display Settings" dialog box opens.

3. Click the Symbols tab.

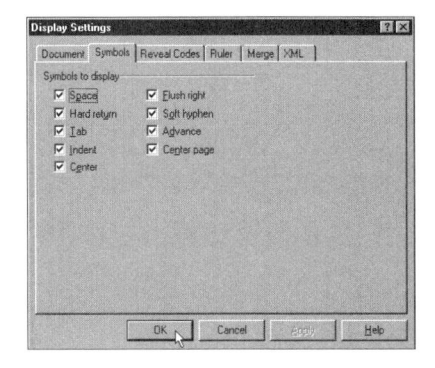

4. Deselect any of the check box options that you don't want displayed when Show ¶ command is activated.

Spell Check

(See "Writing Tools" later in this part.)

Thesaurus

(See "Writing Tools" later in this part.)

Two Page View

This feature lets you see two pages of a document on the screen at one time.

To access it, choose View⇨Two Pages.

TIP

When you use Two Page view in WordPerfect 9, you can edit the text and graphics as you would edit them on a normal-sized page (if you can see the stuff that needs editing). You cannot, however, use Zoom to zoom in on a part of the two-page spread. To use Zoom, you must switch back to Page view or Draft view (see the sections "Draft View" and "Page View" earlier in this part and "Zoom" later in this part).

Undo

This feature restores the document to its previous state before you messed it up.

When you do a boo-boo on the CPU, don't panic. Just remember these little commands:

+ Choose Edit⇨Undo or Redo on the menu bar.
+ Press Ctrl+Z to undo.
+ Press Ctrl+Shift+R to redo.
+ To undo your last action, click the Undo button.
+ To redo your last action, click the Redo button.

TIP: In WordPerfect 9, you can undo (and redo) up to 300 of your past actions (wow!) — although WordPerfect 9 is really only set up to undo the last ten actions when you start using the program. To increase the number of Undos and Redos allowed:

1. Choose Edit⇨Undo/Redo History to open the "Undo/Redo History" dialog box.

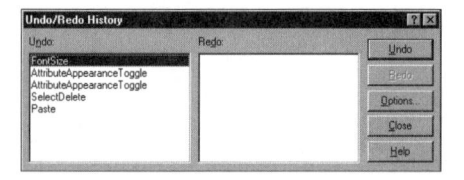

2. Click Options.

3. Enter the new number of Undos/Redos in the "Number of Undo/Redo Items" text box.

4. Consider the option of saving the undo/redo items with the document.

5. Click OK to close the "Undo Options" dialog box.

6. Click Close to shut down the "Undo/Redo History" dialog box.

TIP: To undo more than one action at a time, open the "Undo/Redo History" dialog box, select the last item in the "Undo" list box that you want undone (WordPerfect 9 automatically selects all items above the one you select), and click Undo. To redo more than one item, you perform the same sequence in the "Redo" list box and then click Redo.

Window

The Window commands let you switch between documents that are open in different windows and let you arrange all the open document windows on one screen.

To make another document window active:

1. Click the Window menu.

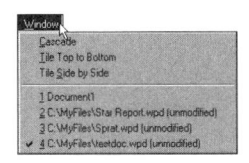

2. Click the number or filename with the mouse.

3. Or to arrange open windows, use these commands:

- **Cascade:** Places the windows one in front of the other with the title bars of each one showing.
- **Tile Top to Bottom:** Places the windows from top to bottom on-screen.
- **Tile Side by Side:** Places the windows side by side on-screen.

TIP
You can have as many as nine windows open if your computer has enough memory.

Writing Tools

WordPerfect 9 comes to you with three powerful tools to keep your writing shipshape:

✦ **Spell Checker:** Checks for misspelled words, duplicate words, and irregular capitalization in documents, parts of documents, and text entry boxes.

✦ **Grammatik:** Proofreads documents, parts of documents, and text entry boxes for grammar and style errors.

✦ **Thesaurus:** Finds synonyms (words that are alike) and antonyms (words that are opposite).

Click the Spell Check button on the WordPerfect 9 toolbar or select any of the tools on the Tools menu.

Spell checking a document

To check the spelling in your document, follow these steps:

1. Position the insertion point in the word or page you want to spell check.

2. Choose Tools⇨Spell Checker or press Ctrl+F1 to select the Spell Checker tab of the "Writing Tools" dialog box.

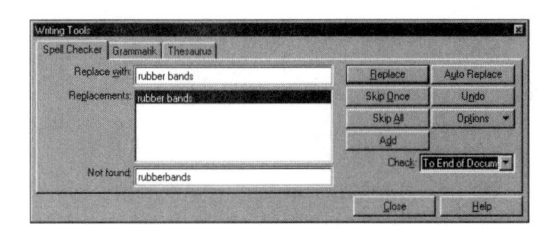

   By default, the program spell checks the entire document (unless text is already selected, in which case the program opts to check only the selection).

3. If you want to change the default, choose from these self-explained commands in the Check scroll list:

   - Word
   - Sentence
   - Paragraph
   - Page
   - Document
   - To End of Document
   - Selected Text
   - Number of Pages

4. Click Start or press Enter to begin spell checking.

   You can have the Spell Checker start checking the document as soon as the Spell Checker opens by choosing Options⇨Auto start. When the Spell Checker locates a word it cannot find in its dictionary, it highlights the word in the text and displays the word in the Not found window. The Spell Checker then provides suggestions for replacing the unknown (and potentially misspelled) word in the "Replacements" list box. The first suggestion in this list is displayed in the Replace with text box.

5. Choose from these options:

- **Click Replace or press Enter:** To replace the unknown word with the word located in the Replace with text box.

- **Select another word in the "Replacements" list box:** After the proposed word appears in the Replace with text box, click Replace or press Enter.

- **Click Skip Once:** To skip the unknown word one time only and continue spell checking.

- **Click Skip All:** To skip this unknown word and every other occurrence of it throughout the document.

- **Click Add:** To add the unknown word to the supplementary spelling dictionary (so that the Spell Checker skips the word in this and every other document).

You can also edit the unknown word while in the text. Click the word in the document to activate the document window, and then make your changes. When you're ready to resume spell checking, click Resume in the "Spell Checker" dialog box.

6. Click Options to display menu commands for configuring the Spell Checker when it encounters duplicate, irregular capitalization, and words with mixed numbers and text.

After the Spell Checker finishes checking the document (or the part you indicated), it displays a Spell Checker alert box informing you that the spell check has been completed and asks whether you want to close the Spell Checker.

7. Click Yes or press Enter to close the "Spell Checker" dialog box and return to the document.

> You can also close the Spell Checker at any time by clicking the Close button in the "Spell Checker" dialog box.

Save your document immediately after spell checking it to ensure that you don't lose the edits made by way of the Spell Checker.

Using Grammatik

Use Grammatik to proofread documents, parts of documents, and text entry boxes for grammar and style errors:

1. Choose Tools⇨Grammatik or press Alt+Shift+F1 to select the Grammatik tab of the "Writing Tools" dialog box.

Writing Tools

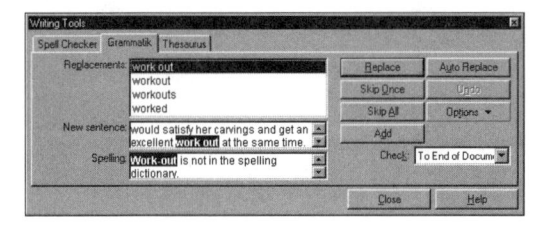

The major parts of the "Grammatik" dialog box function much the same as those of the Spell Checker (see "Spell checking a document" earlier in this part).

2. Click Options⇨Checking Styles to choose a checking style designed for the type of writing you are checking.

3. To create a customized checking style, select Very Strict in the "Checking Styles" list box and then click Edit.

In the "Editing Checking Styles" dialog box, you can create your own grammar checking style.

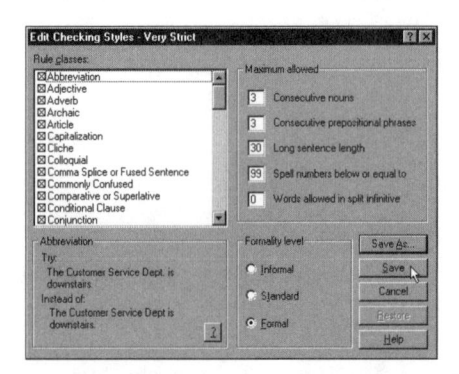

4. When Grammatik finds a grammatical error, the grammar rule and information pertaining to the error appear in the text box at the bottom of the dialog box. You can turn this feature off or on by clicking Turn On Rules on the Options menu.

Writing Tools 59

5. As with the Spell Checker, Grammatik suggests a new sentence in the New sentence text box, and you can apply these options:
   - **Replace:** Replace the sentence with the suggested sentence.
   - **Skip Once:** Skip the error one time.
   - **Skip All:** Skip the error for the rest of the current proofreading session.

6. Click Close in the "Grammatik" dialog box after you're through checking grammar in the document.

TIP: Grammatik also analyzes the grammatical structure of your writing and provides statistics to help you analyze your writing style. Choose Options➪Analysis to access these features.

Using Thesaurus

This feature lets you find synonyms (words with similar meanings) for many of the words you overuse in a document. To look up a word in Thesaurus:

1. Select a word in the current document you want to look up.

2. Choose Tools➪Thesaurus or press Alt+F1 to select the Thesaurus tab of the "Writing Tools" dialog box.

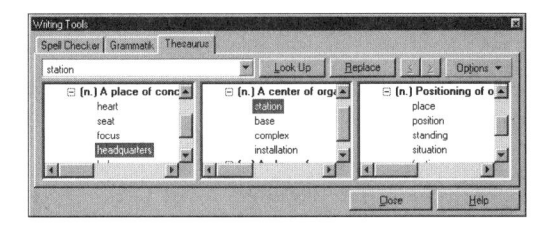

When you start Thesaurus, it automatically looks up the selected word and provides a list of definitions.

3. Click the plus sign (+) next to the definition that best suits your needs to reveal a list of attached synonyms.

If you click on any of the words in this list, another Thesaurus window opens next door, with even more definitions and synonyms. When you find a word you like:

4. Select the word and click the Replace button or double-click the synonym to insert it into the document in place of the old word.

To look up words from the "Thesaurus" dialog box, just type in the text box and click the Look Up button. When you search for a synonym in this manner, the Insert button appears that lets you place your selection at the insertion point in the current document. Use the left and right arrow buttons on the Thesaurus tab to scroll back and forth when there are several Thesaurus windows open.

5. Click Close to return to the open document.

Keep in mind that when you replace a word with a synonym from the Thesaurus, WordPerfect 9 makes no attempt to match the original tense or number in the text. So, if you look up the word *jumped* in a document and select *leap* in the "Thesaurus" dialog box as its replacement, WordPerfect 9 inserts *leap* without an *ed* (which you must then add yourself).

Zoom

This tool lets you change the size of the screen display as you're running WordPerfect 9 in Draft view or Page view.

To open the "Zoom" dialog box:

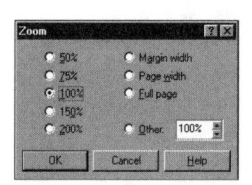

1. Choose View⇨Zoom.

2. Select from these options on the Zoom menu:

- **Margin width:** To have WordPerfect 9 fill the document window with text from margin to margin and with minimal white space.

- **Page width:** To display the entire width of the document within the document window.

- **Full page:** To display the entire length of the document within the document window.

- **Other:** To open the "Zoom" dialog box and set a specific zoom percentage.

Part III

Formatting Documents and Text

One of the ways word processing really advanced our use of the printed word is its capability to let everyone make text that's nice to look at. Gutenberg never had it so good. WordPerfect 9 gives you the means to create a document your way, with just the right look. All the cool techniques for manipulating your document and text are right here in Part III. Enjoy.

In this part . . .

- Fonts and everything you can do to them
- What's justification?
- Much ado about margins
- Indents — hanging, double, and otherwise
- Drop caps (for that Renaissance look)
- Outlines and line numbering
- Styles

Bold

This command formats the selected text in boldface type. To make a section of text bold, follow these steps:

1. Select (highlight) the text you want to be bold.

2. Click the Bold button on the Property bar (See "Property Bar" in Part V) or press Ctrl+B.

To make a section of text bold as you type it, position the insertion point at the place where you want the first bold character to appear before clicking the Bold button or pressing Ctrl+B.

3. Turn off bold by clicking the Bold button again, pressing Ctrl+B, or pressing → once to move beyond the selection.

Bullets and Numbers

This command makes creating bulleted or numbered lists in your document incredibly simple.

Bullets and numbers in a snap

To create a numbered or bulleted list in a document, follow these steps:

1. Position the insertion point at the beginning of the first line on which you want to create a bullet or number.

2. Choose Insert⇨Outline/Bullets & Numbering to open the "Bullets and Numbering" dialog box.

3. Click either the Numbers or Bullets tab, depending on which you want to insert, and choose from the default styles available. You can also select these options:

- **Apply Selected layout to current outline/list:** Changes the current outline/list layout to the layout selected in the Numbers or Bullets Tab.

- **Start new outline/list:** Use to start a new bulleted or numbered list.

- **Insert a new outline/list within the current outline/list:** Inserts a different outline/list layout within the current outline style.

- **Resume numbering from previous outline/list:** Use to resume a numbered list started earlier in the document.

Bullets and Numbers 63

- **Edit:** Use to edit the default bullet, numbering, and outline styles.
- **Create:** Use to create new styles based on your edits.
- **Options:** Use to specify the source of styles for the list; to copy, delete, or reset a style; or to save and retrieve styles.

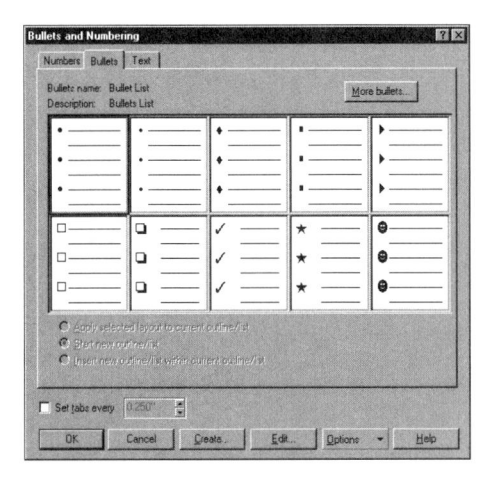

4. Click OK or press Enter.

After you choose the bullet or numbering style, WordPerfect 9 inserts the bullet or first number and indents the insertion point. After you type your first numbered or bulleted text, press Enter and a new bullet or the next number appears in the text.

Getting rid of those bullets

To turn off the automatic bulleting or numbering function, click at the end of the list, and then click the Numbering or Bullets button on the WordPerfect 9 toolbar.

Use the Numbering and Bullets buttons on the WordPerfect 9 toolbar to quickly insert a number or bullet into the text.

To the right of either button is a down arrow that opens a palette of various styles you can apply right away to your bulleted or numbered list:

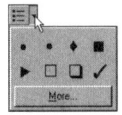

Just click a button to apply that style to your list. The More button on either palette opens the "Bullets and Numbering" dialog box.

Center Line

This command centers a line of text horizontally between the left and right margins.

To keep things centered:

1. Position the insertion point in front of the first character on the line to be centered.

2. Choose Format⇨Line⇨Center or press Shift+F7.

You can quickly apply center line formatting in a number of situations.

- ✦ To center a line before you type it, press Shift+F7 to move the insertion point to the center of the line, type your text, and press Enter. After you press Enter, WordPerfect 9 returns the insertion point to the left margin of the new line.

- ✦ To center a line of existing text, put the insertion point at the beginning of the line and press Shift+F7.

- ✦ To center a bunch of lines, select (highlight) the lines and press Shift+F7.

You can also center text by changing the justification of a document from normal left justification to center justification. For more information about this method, see the "Justification" section later in this part.

Center Page

This feature centers text on a page vertically between the top and bottom margins.

To put the text on your page in the center of things:

1. Choose Format⇨Page⇨Center to open the "Center Page(s)" dialog box.

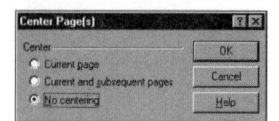

2. Click the appropriate radio button to select one the following options:

- **Current page:** Vertically centers just the text from the current page between the top and bottom margins.

- **Current and subsequent pages:** Vertically centers the current page and all following pages.

- **No centering:** This default setting changes to "Turn Centering Off" after you use the "Current and subsequent pages" radio button to turn vertical centering on.

3. Click OK or press Enter.

Columns

This feature enables you to lay out text in multiple columns.

Creating columns

To display and define your columns by using the "Columns" dialog box, follow these steps:

1. Choose Format⇨Columns to open the "Columns" dialog box.

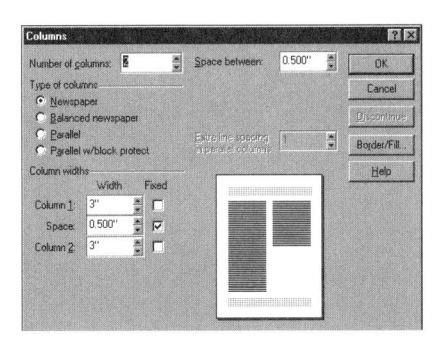

2. Select from the following options:

- **Number of columns:** Use the scroll list buttons or enter the number of newspaper or parallel columns you want to create (between 2 and 32).

- **Type of columns:** Click the radio button next to "Newspaper" when you want the text to be read up and down the columns across the page, next to "Balanced newspaper" when you want WordPerfect 9 to create even newspaper columns, next to

"Parallel" when you want the text to read across and then down the columns, or next to "Parallel w/block protect" when you want parallel columns that always stay together on a page.

- **Space between:** Use "Space between" to change the distance between the columns (0.500 inch by default). If you're creating parallel columns, you can use "Extra line spacing in parallel columns" to increase or decrease, in half-line increments, the number of lines between the parallel columns in your document.

- **Column widths:** Enables you to modify the width of and the space between specific newspaper or parallel columns. (By default, WordPerfect 9 creates uniform columns with the same amount of space between them.) To change the width of a column, choose its text box and enter the width. To change the space between a particular pair of columns, choose its "Space" text box and enter the new distance. Use the "Fixed" check boxes to lock column width and space measurements for specific columns in your document.

3. Click OK or press Enter.

If you create newspaper columns before you type text, keep in mind that you may want to break a column early so that you can continue entering text at the top of the next column. To break the column, click in the next column or press Ctrl+Enter and start typing.

Moving through columns

To move the insertion point between columns:

✦ Press Alt+→ to move one column to the right.

✦ Press Alt+←_to move one column to the left.

You can also use the options in the "Go To" dialog box to move between columns (see the "Go To" section in Part V).

For columns in a hurry:

1. Click the Columns button on the WordPerfect 9 toolbar.

2. Choose the number of newspaper columns (up to five) you want to create from the drop-down list. The drop-down list also provides these options:

- **New Column:** Start a new column at the insertion point.

- **Discontinue:** Turn off newspaper columns later in the document.

- **Format:** Open the "Columns" dialog box to edit columns or change the default "Newspaper" type.

Double Indent

(FAST TRACK) You can adjust the width of your columns by using the Ruler bar (see the "Ruler Bar" section later in this part).

To adjust the width of the columns, click and drag the column margin icons on the tab ruler or the gray guideline between the columns.

(TIP) Rather than trying to deal with parallel columns and their column breaks, try using tables instead (see the "Tables" section in Part VI).

Double Indent

This tool indents the current paragraph one tab stop on both the left and right sides, without making you go through the trouble of changing the left and right margins.

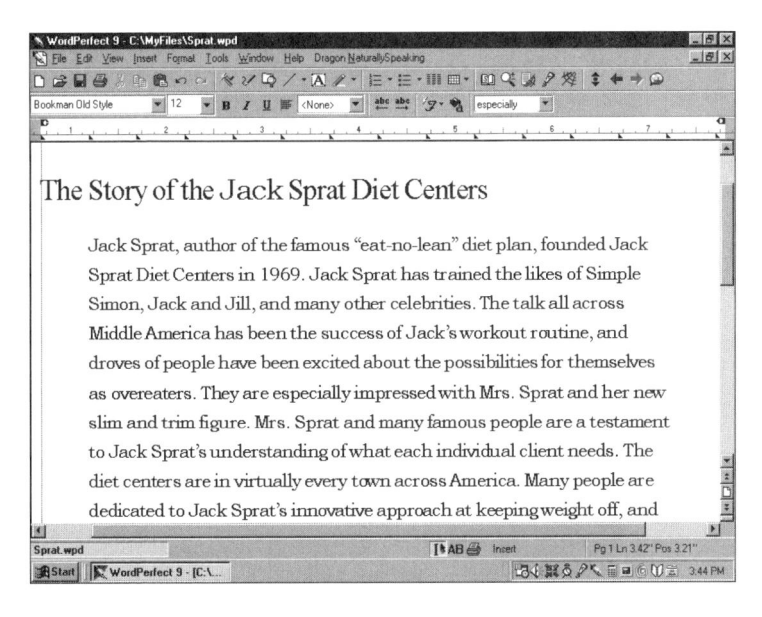

[Screenshot of WordPerfect 9 showing "The Story of the Jack Sprat Diet Centers" document with an indented paragraph about Jack Sprat, author of the famous "eat-no-lean" diet plan.]

The Double Indent feature lets you use a single command to indent a paragraph of text on both sides. (For this reason, it is also known as a left-right indent.) Here's how:

1. Position the insertion point at the beginning of the paragraph.

2. Choose Format⇨Paragraph⇨Double Indent or press Ctrl+Shift+F7.

(WARNING) WordPerfect 9 must be in Insert mode. (Make sure that Typeover has not replaced Insert on the General Status bar located on the right side of the Application Bar at the bottom of the document window.)

Drop Cap

Double Indent is only one of the incredible paragraph-alignment tricks in WordPerfect 9. For more options, *see also* the sections "Hanging Indent" and plain old "Indent" later in this part.

Drop Cap

This tool converts the first character of the current paragraph to a drop cap (you know, that big capital letter that extends halfway down the left side of the paragraph's text).

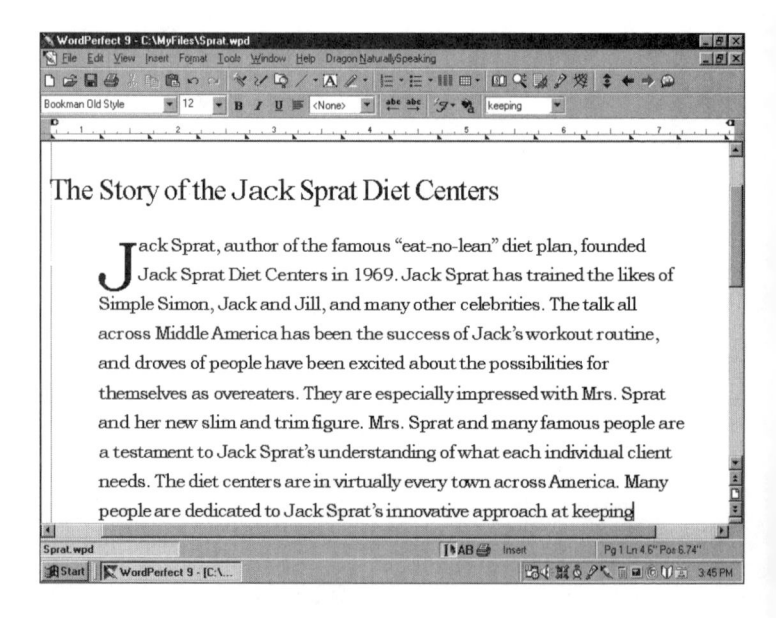

Dropping caps with the pros

The Drop Cap feature lets you fancy-up the first paragraph of your document with a drop cap (just like you see in those highfalutin' coffee table books). To do so:

1. Type the text of your paragraph.

2. Choose Format⇨Paragraph⇨Drop Cap or press Ctrl+Shift+C.

WordPerfect 9 then converts the very first letter in the paragraph to a drop cap, and the Drop Cap Property Bar appears.

Customizing drop caps

You can use the buttons on the Drop Cap Property Bar to customize the size and position of the drop cap as shown in the following table.

Icon	Button Name	Function
	Drop Cap Style	Lets you select a new drop cap style from the pop-up palette or remove the drop cap by clicking the No Cap button (the one with the X icon).
	Drop Cap Size	Lets you select the number of lines you want the drop cap to take up.
	Drop Cap Position	Lets you change the position of the drop cap in relation to the margin and the paragraph text below the drop cap.
	Drop Cap Font	Lets you select a new font and font attribute for the drop cap in the "Drop Cap Font" dialog box (which works just like the regular "Font Properties" dialog box — see the "Font" section later in this part).
	Drop Cap Border/Fill	Lets you specify a new border and/or fill pattern for the drop cap in the "Drop Cap Border" dialog box (which works just like all the other "Border" dialog boxes in WordPerfect 9).
	Drop Cap Options	Lets you specify other options for your drop cap, such as: "Number of characters in drop cap" (use the scroll list to enter the number of characters in the drop cap), "Make first whole word as drop cap" (converts the entire first word to drop caps), "Wrap text around drop cap" (the default, which you rarely, if ever, change), "Adjust for diacritic marks" (moves the drop cap down slightly to accommodate the letter's diacritical mark — the accent mark that accompanies some of the alphabets our European cousins use), and "Adjust for descender" (lets letters in the paragraph text wrap around drop cap letters that extend below the baseline).

After you finish creating and customizing your drop cap, you can click in the document (away from the drop cap) to hide the Drop Cap Property Bar.

Flush Right

Aligns a short line of text flush with the right margin. Here's how:

1. Position the insertion point in front of the first character of the line to be flush right.

2. Choose Format⇨Line⇨Flush Right or press Alt+F7.

70 Font

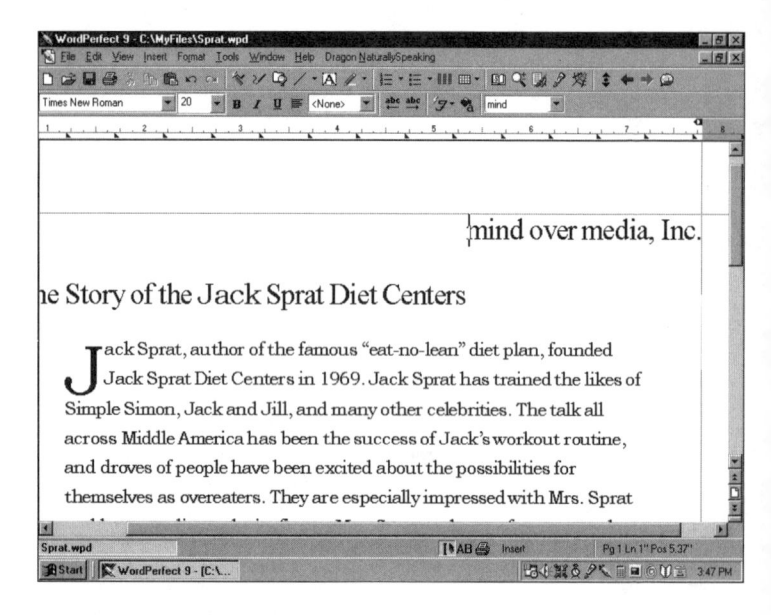

[FAST TRACK]

You can quickly apply flush right formatting in a number of situations, as follows:

+ **Single line of text:** Position the insertion point at the beginning of the single line of text you want aligned with the right margin (the line must end with a hard return), then press Alt+F7.

+ **Align a new line of text:** Press Alt+F7, type the text, and press Enter. The insertion point returns to the left margin as soon as you press Enter.

+ **Align several short lines:** Select the lines and press Alt+F7.

[TIP]

You can also right-align text by changing the justification of the document from the normal left justification to right justification. For more information about this method, see the "Justification" section later in this part.

Font

WordPerfect 9 lets you change the font, font size, appearance, position, relative size, and color of new text.

Using the "Font Properties" dialog box

You access all of WordPerfect's font formatting features using the "Font Properties" dialog box.

1. Position the insertion point at the beginning of the text where the change is to take place.

If you want to apply the font or font attribute to only a portion of the existing text (such as a heading), first select the text (see the "Select (Text)" section in Part II) and then choose your options in the "Font Properties" dialog box.

2. Choose the Font command on the menu bar or press F9 to open the "Font Properties" dialog box.

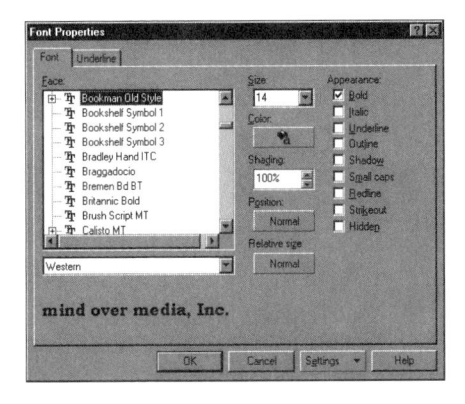

3. Select from the following options on the Font tab:

- **Face:** Lets you choose a new font from the scroll list. Click the plus (+) sign to the left of the font types to expand the directory tree of available fonts and choose among Regular, Italic, Bold, and Bold Italic styles for that type.

- **Size:** Lets you choose a new point size for the font from the scroll window. If the size you want to use isn't listed, you can type the point size in the Size text box.

- **Color:** Lets you specify a new color for the font you selected. To choose a new color, click the Color button and then choose a color from the pop-up color palette. To define a custom color for the color palette, choose the More button and then use the "Select Color" dialog box.

- **Shading:** To choose a new shading for the color, enter a new percentage or use the scroll buttons in the Shading scroll list.

- **Position:** Lets you choose among Normal, Superscript, and Subscript as the vertical position of the font you selected.

- **Relative size:** Enables you to choose a new size for your font (Fine, Small, Normal, Large, Very Large, and Extra Large), based entirely on a set percentage of the size of the initial font. Large is 120 percent bigger than Normal, for example. If the initial font for your printer is 10-point Courier, choosing Large gives you 12-point Courier because this size is 120 percent of the 10-point initial font.
- **Appearance:** Provides multiple appearance options for the font you choose, including Bold, Italic, Underline, Outline, Shadow, Small caps, Redline, Strikeout, and Hidden.

Select from the following options on the Underline tab:

- **Apply to:** By default, the "Text & Spaces" radio button is selected; when you're underlining in WordPerfect 9, the program underlines the spaces between words. To remove underlining from the spaces, click the "Text Only" radio button. To add underlining between tabs, choose the "Text and Tabs" radio button.
- **Line Style:** Choose from the selection of line styles or turn underlining off.
- **Color:** Lets you specify a new color for the underline style you have selected. To choose a new color, click the "Color" button and then choose the color from the pop-up color palette. To define a custom color for the color palette, choose the More button and then use the "Select Color" dialog box. Use the "Same as text" check box to apply the color selected for text on the Font tab of the "Font Properties" dialog box.

5. Click the Settings button to choose from the following commands:

- **Set face and point size as default for this document:** Automatically apply the selected font face, size, style, and attributes for the current document and printer.
- **Set face and point size as default for all documents:** Automatically apply the selected font face, size, style, and attributes for all documents you create.
- **Edit Font Mapping:** Change the fonts that are automatically selected when you choose a new Relative size option. (See "Relative size" earlier in this list.)

6. Choose OK to close the "Font Properties" dialog box.

Turning everything off!

The new font face, size, style, and attributes you choose stay in effect from the insertion point's position at the time of the change until you turn them off. To turn off a font change, you must choose the original font in the Font Properties dialog box. To turn off a size change, you must select the original size in the "Font Properties" dialog box.

To turn off a color change, you must select the original color (usually black) in the Text color area of the "Font Properties" dialog box. To turn off appearance changes, open the "Font Properties" dialog box and deselect all the Appearance options. To turn off a relative size change, select the Normal setting for the Relative size option in the "Font Properties" dialog box.

> **TIP**
> You can also turn off such appearance attributes as bold, italics, and underlining by choosing that attribute again. Press Ctrl+B, Ctrl+I, or Ctrl+U, respectively.

Or click the Bold, Italic, or Underline button on the WordPerfect 9 toolbar.

> **TIP**
> If you select your text (see the "Select (Text)" section in Part II for details) and then make any of the changes offered in the "Font Properties" dialog box, WordPerfect 9 automatically turns off these attributes at the end of the selection. This way, you don't have to remember to do so yourself.

> **FAST TRACK**
> You can make lightning fast changes to a font's face and size using font tools on the Property bar. See "Property Bar" in Part V and "RealTime Preview" in the next section.

RealTime Preview

> **WORDPERFECT 9 New!**
> RealTime Preview is a new feature in WordPerfect 9 that lets you preview font changes before you commit yourself to them. You can see what your actual text will look like if you add formatting features to it. Here's how it works:

1. Click in a paragraph to insert the cursor or select the text you want to edit.

When you click to insert the cursor in a paragraph rather than select specific text, formatting occurs from the insertion point to the end of the paragraph.

2. Click the "Font Face" list box on the Property Bar.

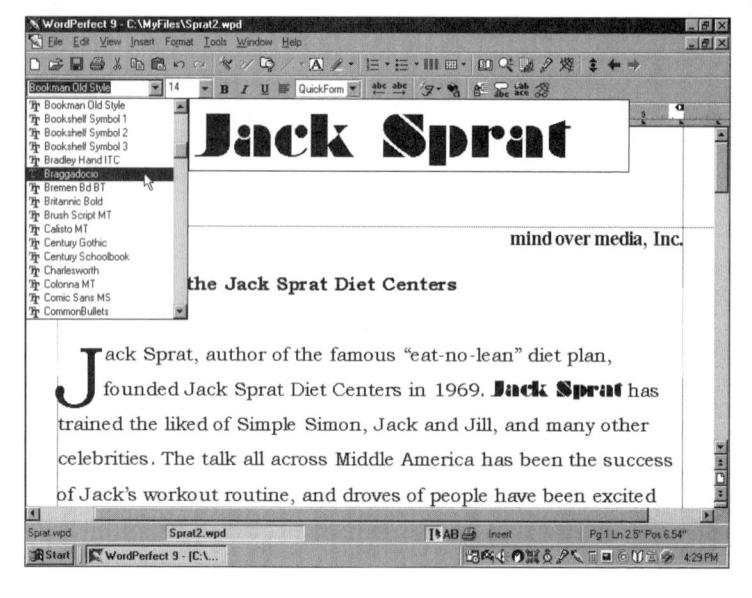

3. Point to a font to preview it.

When you pause on a font, a preview of the text in that font appears in a preview window to the right of the list box. You also see how the font change affects the text in the document window.

4. Click the font in the list box to apply the font.

RealTime Preview works in exactly the same manner when using the "Font Size" list box on the Property bar.

To use RealTime Preview on a single word or phrase, just select the word or phrase prior to previewing.

For more information about these features, see Chapter 6 of *WordPerfect 9 For Windows For Dummies*.

Hanging Indent

This feature sets off the first line of an indented paragraph by releasing it to the left margin.

Indent 75

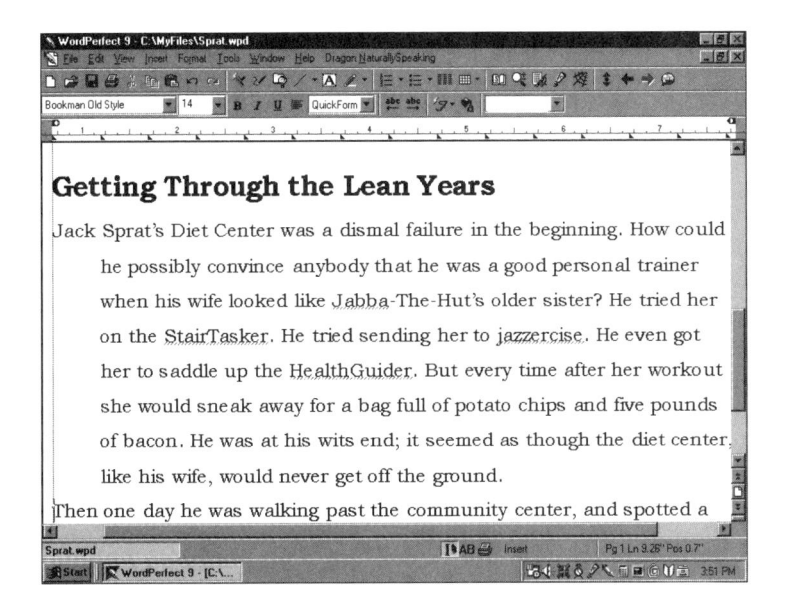

To add this flourish to your documents:

1. Place the insertion point at the beginning of the first line of the paragraph.

2. Choose Format➪Paragraph➪Hanging Indent or press Ctrl+F7.

> **TIP**
> You can also create a hanging indent by pressing the Tab key at the beginning of any line in the paragraph except the first line.

> **WARNING**
> Be sure that the insertion point is at the beginning of the first line of the paragraph before you choose the Hanging Indent command. Otherwise, the results are not pretty. For other indenting possibilities with WordPerfect 9, *see also* "Double Indent" earlier in this part and "Indent," which follows.

Indent

This command moves the left edge of an entire paragraph one tab stop to the right, creating an indent that sets the paragraph off from normal text.

To give your documents that high school assignment look:

1. Place the insertion point at the beginning of the first line of the paragraph.

2. Choose Format➪Paragraph➪Indent, or press F7.

76 Justification

WARNING: Be sure that the insertion point is at the very beginning of the paragraph before you indent it, unless you happen to like indents in the middle of a paragraph.

For information about the other types of indents that are possible with WordPerfect 9, *see also* the "Double Indent" and "Hanging Indent" sections earlier in this part.

Justification

This set of commands changes the way paragraphs are aligned in a document.

Button	Name	Keyboard Shortcut	What It Does
Left	Align Left	Ctrl+L	Flush left, ragged right margin
Right	Align Right	Ctrl+R	Flush right, ragged left margin
Center	Center	Ctrl+E	Centers all lines between the left and right margins
Full	Full	Ctrl+J	Flush left and flush right margin
All	All	N/A	Forces justification even in the last, short line of each paragraph so that the line is flush left and right, like all the other full lines

Line Numbering

This tool numbers the lines on each page of your document.

Great for spelling tests! Here's how:

1. Place the insertion point at the beginning of the line you want to number.

2. Choose Format⇨Line⇨Numbering to open the Line Numbering dialog box.

Line Numbering 77

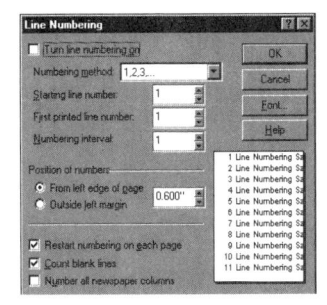

Choose from these available options:

- **Turn line numbering on:** Lets you turn line numbering on and off at the current position of the insertion point. If this check box has a check mark in it, line numbering is turned on; if the check box is empty, line numbering is off.

- **Numbering method:** Chooses a new numbering method from the following: Number (the default), Lowercase Letter, Uppercase Letter, Lowercase Roman, or Uppercase Roman.

- **Starting line number:** Changes the starting line (1 is the default).

- **First printed line number:** Chooses the first line number to be printed in the document (1 is the default).

- **Numbering interval:** Changes the interval between the numbers printed in the document (1 is the default).

- **Position of numbers:** Changes the position of the line numbers. You can choose whether you want the distance to be measured "From left edge of page" or "Outside left margin."

- **Restart numbering on each page:** Enables WordPerfect 9 to restart the numbering (from the Starting line number) on each new page of the document.

- **Count blank lines:** Determines whether blank lines are counted in the line numbering (they are, by default).

- **Number all newspaper columns:** Determines whether each newspaper column on the page gets line numbers.

- **Font:** Allows you to choose new fonts, attributes, and colors for the line numbers.

3. Click OK or press Enter.

Margins

This option lets you set new left, right, top, and bottom margins for your document.

To change margins:

1. Position the insertion point on the line on which the new left and right margins will take effect or on the page on which the new top and bottom margins will take effect. The margin change will affect subsequent paragraphs or pages.

2. Choose Format⇨Margins or press Ctrl+F8 to open the Margins/Layout tab of the "Page Setup" dialog box.

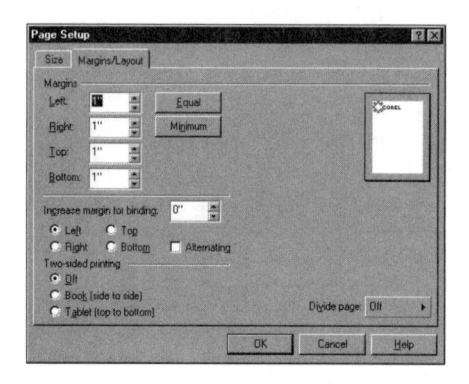

3. Select the margin text box you want to change (Left, Right, Top, or Bottom).

4. Enter the new margin setting or select it with the scroll list buttons located to the right of the text box.

5. Click OK or press Enter.

You can change the left and right margins quickly by dragging the left and right margin guidelines (gray dotted lines) in the document window or by dragging the margin icons located on the Ruler bar. The top and bottom margin guidelines also function this way. Double-clicking on the margin icons opens the Margins/Layout tab on the "Page Setup" dialog box.

Outline

This tool creates outlines in your document just like those your teacher had you make.

Creating an outline

You can use the outline feature to create formal outlines that would make your English teacher proud. When you create a formal outline, you can have as many as eight successive outline levels. WordPerfect 9 automatically numbers and formats the entries in each level for you according to the outline style you choose. To begin organizing your great thoughts, follow these steps:

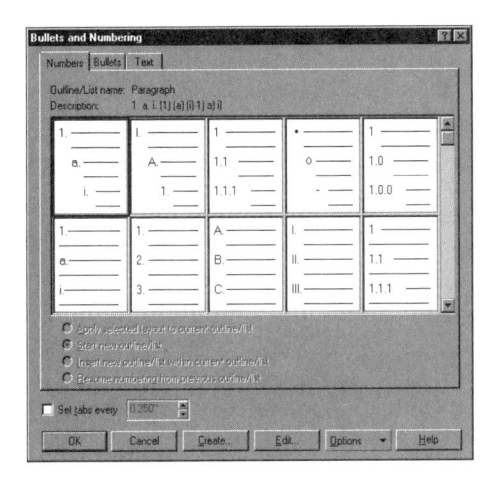

1. Position the insertion point at the beginning of the line where you want the initial first-level heading of your outline to appear (usually on the first line after the one that contains the name of your outline).

2. Choose Insert⇨Outline/Bullets and Numbering on the menu bar.

3. Select an outline numbering style on the Numbers tab of the "Bullets and Numbering" dialog box.

4. Click OK or press Enter.

See "Bullets and Numbers" earlier in this part for more on this dialog box.

WordPerfect 9 inserts the first outline number or letter(1., I., A. and so on), indents the insertion point to the first tab stop, and displays the Outline Property Bar. (The big, fat 1 you see in the left margin merely indicates that this is a first-level heading.) If you can't see the big, fat 1 in the margin, you need to click the "Show Icons" button on the Outline Property Bar.

5. Type the text of the initial first-level heading and then press Enter.

WordPerfect 9 inserts the second outline number (2.) and indents the insertion point so that you can enter the second first-level heading (indicated by the big, fat 1 in the left margin).

6. To do another first-level heading, type the second first-level heading and press Enter. If, instead, you want to enter the initial second-level heading, press Tab to change the outline level (and change the 2. to an a. and the big, fat 1 in the left margin to a big, fat 2). Then type the initial second-level heading and press Enter.

WordPerfect 9 enters the next number (or letter) in sequence for whatever outline level is current. Use the following keys to navigate to different heading levels:

- **Enter:** Press Enter to terminate each level after entering the heading.

- **Tab:** To enter a heading for the next-lower level, press Tab to move to the next outline level before entering the heading.

- **Shift+Tab:** To enter a heading at a higher level, press Shift+Tab until you move up the levels sufficiently before entering the heading. (Remember that the outline levels are indicated by the big, fat numbers in the left margin.)

7. After you finish entering the last heading for your outline, press Enter and Backspace to convert the last outline number or letter to text (indicated by the big, fat T in the left margin).

The Outline Property Bar disappears when you move from outline numbering to text. If you have margin icons showing, the only way to turn them off is to click in the outline to open the Outline Property Bar, click the Show Icons button to disable the feature, and then click outside the outline to continue typing text.

Using the Outline Property Bar

When you work with an outline, you can use the buttons on the Outline Property Bar to make short work of your outline changes.

Redline/Strikeout

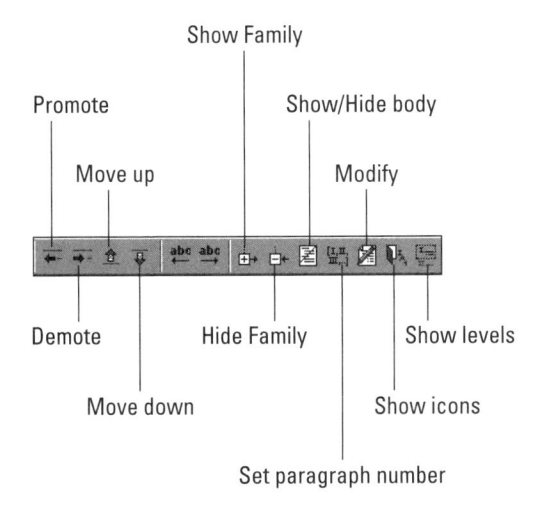

Diagram of the Outline Property Bar with labeled buttons:
- Promote
- Move up
- Demote
- Move down
- Show Family
- Hide Family
- Show/Hide body
- Modify
- Set paragraph number
- Show icons
- Show levels

You can use the various buttons on the Outline Property Bar to perform just about anything that can be done to an outline.

Button Name	What It Does
Promote	Changes the active outline item to the previous level
Demote	Changes the active outline item to the next level
Move Up	Moves the active or selected item or family up while keeping the same family
Move Down	Moves the active or selected item or family down while keeping the same family
Show Family	Shows the family of an outline item
Hide Family	Can you guess? Hides the family of an outline item
Show/Hide Body	Shows or hides the body of text, not a Hitchcock Theater episode
Set Paragraph Number	Sets the paragraph number to a specific value
Modify	Changes the outline appearance and creates a new style based on changes
Show Icons	Shows outline icons (the big fat numbers) in the left margin
Show Levels	Shows outline levels

Redline/Strikeout

(See "Font" earlier in this part.)

Ruler Bar

The Ruler bar shows the current settings of the tabs and the left and right margins at the insertion point. You can also manipulate the tab and margin icons to change these settings.

To show the Ruler bar choose View⇨Ruler or press Alt+Shift+F3.

Clicking ruler parts

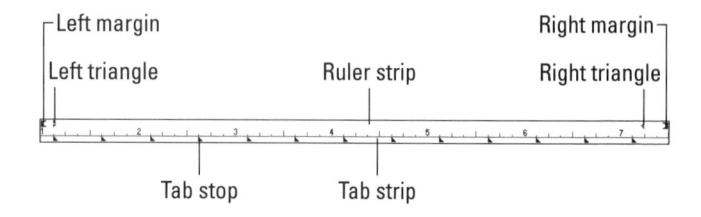

```
 ┌Left margin                              Right margin┐
 │Left triangle          Ruler strip       Right triangle│
 ├─────┬─────┬─────┬─────┬─────┬─────┬─────┤
       2     3     4     5     6     7
          Tab stop   Tab strip
```

Besides showing your basic ruler type things, the Ruler bar doubles as a great page setup utility, as you see when you double-click the parts shown in the following table.

Part	Why Double-Click It
Ruler strip	To open the Ruler tab of the "Settings" dialog box
Tab strip or Tab stop	To display the "Tab Set" dialog box
Margin strip	To open the "Margins" dialog box

Using the margin icons and tab stops

Click and drag these Ruler bar parts to work magic on margins, indents, and tabs:

- **Margin icon (left or right):** Drag to change left or right margin settings.

- **Triangle (left or right):** Drag to change the left or right indent of the paragraphs. The left triangle is comprised of two parts — top and bottom — that move together or separately (see each discussed separately under "Left top triangle" and "Left bottom triangle" later in this list).

- **Left top triangle:** Drag to change the indent of the first line of the paragraph.

- **Left bottom triangle:** Drag to change the indent of all but the first line of the paragraph. Creates a hanging indent.

Styles 83

+ **Tab stop:** Drag to a new position on the tab ruler to change a tab setting. Drag the icon off the tab ruler to remove a tab setting. To add a tab, just click in the tab ruler where you want the tab added.

> **FAST TRACK**
>
> To add a different style of tab, select the type of tab (<u>L</u>eft, <u>C</u>enter, <u>R</u>ight, <u>D</u>ecimal, ...<u>L</u>eft, ...<u>Ce</u>nter, ...<u>R</u>ight, or ...Deci<u>m</u>al) on the Ruler bar QuickMenu and then click the place on the tab ruler where you want this tab to be added.

Styles

These tools let you format various parts of a document in the same manner by simply applying the appropriate style to the text. By using styles, you don't have to use individual formatting commands every time you format text.

Styles à la QuickStyle

The easiest way to create the style is by example, using the QuickStyle feature, as shown in these steps:

1. Format the document text exactly as you want it to appear in the style, including fonts, sizes, attributes, alignment, justification, and so on.

2. Select the formatted text. Be sure to include as part of your selection all the secret codes that change the font or font size or otherwise format this selected text! See "Reveal Codes" in Part VIII for more on this cryptic WordPerfect feature.

3. Choose Format⇨Styles (or press Alt+F8) to open the "Styles" dialog box.

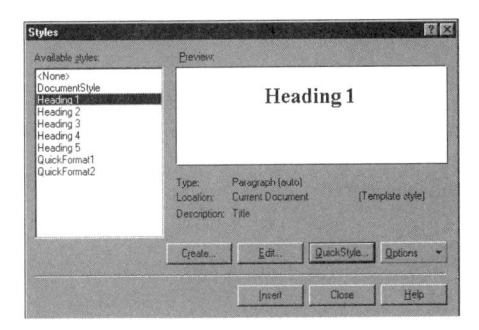

4. Click QuickStyle to open the "QuickStyle" dialog box.

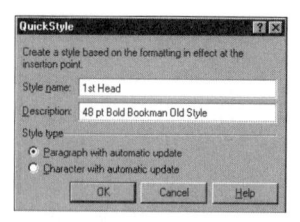

5. Enter a name for your new style (such as 1st Head) in the Style name text box. Then press Tab.

The name can be as long as 12 characters.

6. Enter a description of the new style in the Description text box.

7. By default, WordPerfect 9 creates a Paragraph style. This means that the program applies the formatting to the entire paragraph. To create a Character style instead (the program applies the formatting to only the selected text), choose the "Character with automatic update" radio button.

8. Click OK or press Enter to close the "QuickStyle" dialog box and return to the Styles dialog box.

Your new style is now listed and selected.

9. To apply your brand-new style to the text that is currently selected in the document, click Insert. To close the "Styles" dialog box without assigning the style to the selected text, click Close.

Turning on a style before you type the text

1. Position the insertion point in the text where you want the style formatting to begin.

2. Open the "Styles" dialog box by choosing Format⇨Styles or pressing Alt+F8.

3. Select the style in the list box.

4. Click Insert.

Now you can type the text.

Turning off the style in a new paragraph

1. Open the "Styles" dialog box by choosing Format⇨Styles or by pressing Alt+F8.

2. Select \<None\> in the list box.

3. Click Insert.

Applying a paragraph style to an existing paragraph of text

1. Position the insertion point somewhere in the paragraph to which you want to apply the style.
2. Open the "Styles" dialog box by choosing Format➪Styles or by pressing Alt+F8.
3. Select the style in the "Available styles" list box found in the "Styles" dialog box.
4. Click Insert.

For more information about this command, see Chapter 11 of *WordPerfect 9 For Windows For Dummies*.

Tab Set

This tool lets you change the tabs in your document.

You can change tabs directly on the Ruler bar (see the "Ruler Bar" section earlier in this part for details). You can also double-click any of the tab icons on the Ruler bar to display the "Tab Set" dialog box and change the tabs.

You can change tabs anywhere in the document text. To set uniform tabs for the document, follow these steps:

1. Position the insertion point somewhere in the first paragraph where the new tab settings will take effect.
2. Choose Format➪Line➪Tab Set to open the "Tab Set" dialog box.

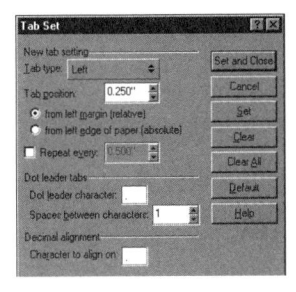

3. Choose from these available options:
   - **Clear All:** Delete all the current tabs.
   - **Tab type:** Select the type of tabs you want to set.

Tab Set

- **Tab position:** Enter the distance from the first tab to the left margin or to the left edge of the page. You can also select this distance with the scroll list buttons. Zero inches puts the first tab in line with the left margin.

- **Repeat every:** Put a check mark in this check box and, using the text box, enter a measurement for how far apart each tab stop should be. You can also select this measurement with the scroll list buttons.

- **From left edge of paper (absolute):** Select this radio button if you want the tabs to always remain fixed, even if you change the left margin.

- **From left margin (relative):** This setting is the default setting.

- **Dot leader character:** Change the dot leader character when you're using a dot leader tab (such as Dot Left, Dot Center, Dot Right, or Dot Decimal). Enter the new character in the text box. To insert a character not available from the keyboard, press Ctrl+W and choose the WordPerfect Character (see the "WordPerfect Characters" section later in this part).

- **Spaces between characters:** Change the spacing between each dot (or other leader you may have specified). Enter the new distance in the text box (or you can select this measurement with the scroll list buttons).

- **Set:** Click this button to display your tab settings on the Ruler bar without closing the "Tab Set" dialog box.

- **Character to align on:** Change the alignment character when you're setting Decimal or Dot Decimal tabs (for example, lining up dollar figures in a column). Enter the new alignment character in the text box.

4. Click Set and Close or press Enter to close the "Tab Set" dialog box and return to your document.

   You can now see your new uniform tab settings.

TIP: You can also set individual tab settings in the "Tab Set" dialog box. Simply choose the type of tab and enter its position (relative to the left margin or the left edge of the paper) in the Tab position text box. Then click Set and Close to insert the tab on the tab ruler.

CROSS-REFERENCE: For more information about this command, see Chapter 8 of *WordPerfect 9 For Windows For Dummies*.

Typeover

Typeover is the typing mode opposite the default typing mode, which is Insert. In Typeover mode, the new characters you type on a line eat up the existing characters rather than push the existing characters to the right of the newly typed text (as is the case when you're using Insert mode).

To switch between insert and typeover modes, press the Insert key on your keyboard. WordPerfect 9 always tells you when you have switched into Typeover mode by replacing Insert with Typeover on the General Status bar.

Underline

This tool underlines selected text in the document. To emphasize text thusly:

1. Select the important text.

2. Click the Underline button on the WordPerfect 9 toolbar.

You can underline text before or after you type it, just as you can with bold and italics (see the "Bold" section earlier in this part to get the general idea).

WordPerfect Characters

You can insert special and sometimes weird characters that are not available from the regular keyboard (such as foreign language, math, and science symbols).

To insert a WordPerfect character into the text of your document or into a text box in a dialog box, follow these steps:

1. Position the insertion point where you want the character to appear.

2. Choose Insert⇨Symbol or press Ctrl+W to open the "Symbols" dialog box. (You must press Ctrl+W when you're in a dialog box.)

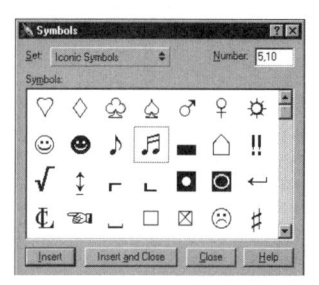

3. Choose the character set you want to use in the Set pop-up list (the default is Iconic Symbols).

That is, click the button in the Set area to open the list and then click the character set you want.

4. Click the character to use in the "Symbols" list box.

5. Click Insert (or double-click the character) to insert the selected character and leave the "Symbols" dialog box open.

6. Click Insert and Close to insert the selected character and also close the dialog box.

Each WordPerfect character is assigned a set number plus a character number. This number appears in the Number text box when you select a character in the "Symbols" list box. If you already know the set number and character number for the character you want to use, select it by simply entering the two numbers in the Number text box, separated by a comma.

Part IV

Printing Your Documents

Whoever thought that computers would create a paperless society was dreaming. How could anybody take the time to make a document look so darn good and then leave it on a computer desktop so that only people who know a PDF from a CD-ROM can enjoy it? If you must know, PDFs or portable document files, are electronic files (now there's a good term) that can be moved from one computer to another while maintaining their formatting regardless of platform or software considerations. Sorry you asked, right?

Thankfully, at this point in time (but maybe not for long if the PDF people have anything to say about it), printing is king. Part IV is all about printing your documents so that the rest of us can enjoy them.

In this part . . .

- ✔ Printing made easy
- ✔ Paper size considerations
- ✔ Merging data for printing purposes
- ✔ Envelopes
- ✔ Labels
- ✔ Junk mail

Envelope

This feature lets you quickly address an envelope for a letter that's in the document editing window. When you use the Envelope feature, WordPerfect 9 locates the mailing address in the letter and automatically copies it to the Mailing Address area of a new envelope that appears in the document window below your letter. The Envelope Property Bar also displays above the document window.

To have WordPerfect 9 do everything but lick the stamp, follow these steps:

1. Open a letter that contains a mailing address in the document window.

2. Choose Format➪Envelope.

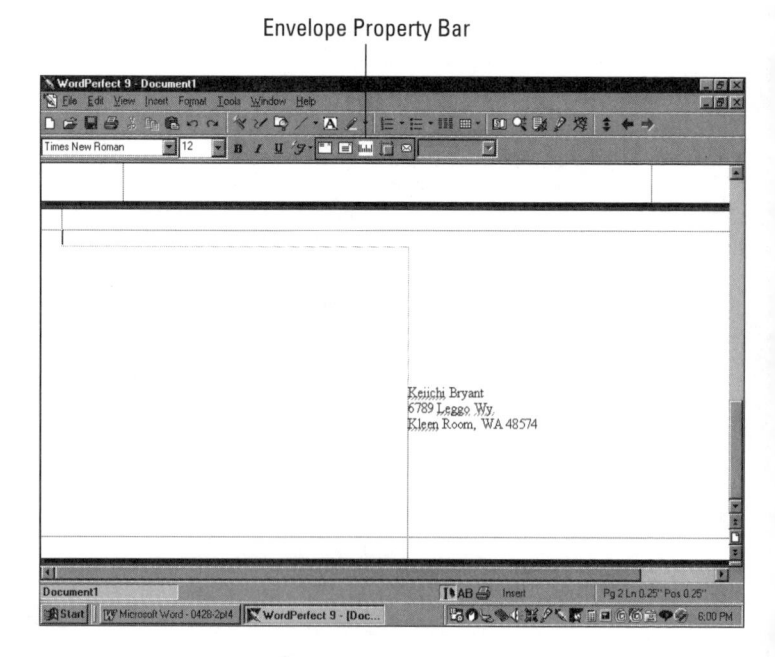

Envelope Property Bar

3. Choose from these available options on the Envelope Property Bar:

- **Return Address:** Lets you enter or edit the return address to be printed on the envelope.

- **Mailing Address:** Lets you edit the mailing address that was chosen from the letter that appears in the current document window, or enter a mailing address if none can be located in the current document.
- **Bar Code:** Creates a POSTNET bar code to be printed on the envelope. See "Bar Code" in Part VIII for more on this feature.
- **Envelope Positions:** Lets you modify the positions of the return and mailing addresses.
- **Envelope Size:** Lets you choose the envelope size you want to use. The 4.125-inch x 9.5-inch business envelope is selected by default.

To print envelopes:

4. Position the cursor on the page of your document that contains the envelope and choose File⇨Print.

For more information about this command, see Chapter 17 of *WordPerfect 9 For Windows For Dummies*.

Insert Filename

This feature lets you insert the document's filename into your document. You can use this nifty feature to add the filename to your header or footer so that you can cross-reference the printout with its disk file.

To use this feature:

1. Click to place the insertion point where you want the filename inserted.

2. Choose Insert⇨Other⇨Filename.

To insert the filename plus its entire directory path (starting with C: or whatever the heck the drive letter is):

1. Click to place the insertion point where you want the filename and directory path inserted.

2. Choose Insert⇨Other⇨Path and Filename from this cascading menu.

Labels

This tool formats address labels so that you can use the labels to send mass mailings.

Mass quantities of labels

To set up labels follow these steps:

1. Choose Format⇨Labels to open the "Labels" dialog box.

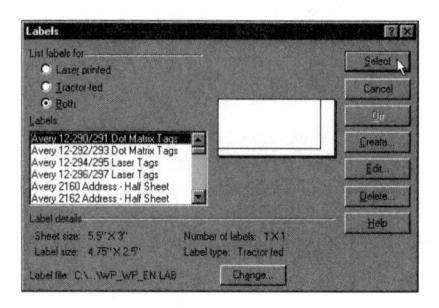

2. Choose from the following options:

- **List labels for:** Lets you choose which types of label definitions are displayed in the "Labels" list box. Choose Laser printed, Tractor-fed, or Both (the default).

- **Labels:** Lets you use the associated list box to choose by name the type of labels to use. When you choose a label in this list, the program displays the sheet size, label size, number of labels on a sheet, and the label type in the Label details area of the "Labels" dialog box. WordPerfect also displays the selected label definition in the Label file area.

- **Change:** Lets you select, create, or edit a new file of label definitions for use with your printer. The file you select here appears after Label File in the Label file area of the "Labels" dialog box (by default, this file is wp_wp_us.lab).

- **Select:** Selects the labels highlighted in the "Labels" list box.

- **Off:** Turns off labels in a document and returns you to the normal paper size and type for your printer (usually letter size).

- **Create:** Lets you create a new label definition if none of the predefined labels are suitable.

- **Edit:** Lets you modify the predefined label definition that's selected in the "Labels" list box.

- **Delete:** Lets you delete the label definition selected in the "Labels" list box.

Merge

3. After you finish selecting a label for printing, click Select to close the "Labels" dialog box and return to the document window.

Editing labels in the document window

When you select a label form that has multiple labels on a single physical page, WordPerfect 9 treats each label as its own page on-screen. In other words, the Page indicator changes as you go from label to label. To move around while editing labels:

✦ **Press Ctrl+Enter:** To begin filling in a new label (Ctrl+Enter is a hard page break).

✦ **Press Alt+PgDn or Alt+PgUp:** To move from page to page.

mind over media, Inc 65 3rd St., Suite 21 Pt. Reyes Station, CA 94956	Marla Sachiko 576 Palomino Lane Chestnut, MI 98889	Keiichi Bryant 409 Leggo St. Kleen Room, NJ 9876
Kina Nokibo 4903 Akita Lane Dogtown, OH 98888	Kisa Otanashi Neko 6793 Kibble Dr. Snootycat, NY 98765	Michael Bryant 1569 Chef's Circle El Queso Grande, TX
Suzette Hunt 58934 Watercolor St. Angelheart, NE 83487		

To see how each individual label looks, make sure that the program is in Page view rather than in Draft view.

CROSS-REFERENCE

For more information about labels, see Chapter 17 of *WordPerfect 9 For Windows For Dummies*.

Merge

This feature generates personalized form letters and other documents that consist of canned text plus variable information. This variable information is dropped in from a *data file*. Before you can perform a merge, you have to create a data file and a *form file*.

Creating a table data file

A data file contains the data records you want to use in the merge (such as the names and addresses of clients). The easiest way to create a data file is to set it up as a table:

Merge

1. Choose Tools⇨Merge or press Shift+F9 to open the "Merge" dialog box.

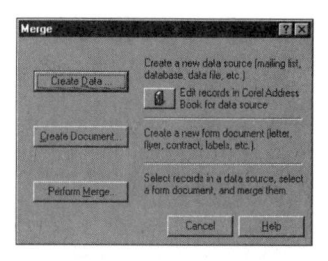

The "Merge" dialog box contains the following options:

- **Create Data:** Creates a file with names, addresses, or other information to merge with a form file.

- **Create Document:** Creates a form file to control the merged output. For example, to create a letter, insert field codes, and then merge with an associated data source.

- **Perform Merge:** Performs the merge. You can specify which files you want to merge, specify the location of the merged output, select specific records from the data source, and choose other merge options.

2. To begin creating a data file, click Create Data.

To create a data file, you must first name the fields (the smallest units) in the data file. For example, you may name the fields Last Name, First Name, Street Address, and so on.

If the current document is not empty, the "Create Merge File" dialog box appears with the "Use file in active window" radio button selected.

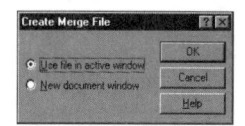

3. Click OK or press Enter to create the data file in the current document window, or choose the "New document window" radio button to create the data file in a new document window before you click OK or press Enter.

WordPerfect 9 then displays the "Create Data File" dialog box in which you name the fields (pieces of information) you want to use in the new data file.

4. For each field you want, enter a descriptive name for that field in the Name a field text box. Press Enter or click Add after typing each field name to add it to the "Field Name" list box.

5. After you finish adding field names, click OK or press Enter to close the "Create Data File" dialog box.

After closing the "Create Data File" dialog box, WordPerfect 9 automatically opens the "Quick Data Entry" dialog box.

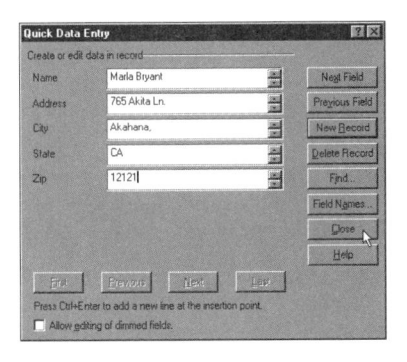

6. Fill out the first record in the "Quick Data Entry" dialog box by entering information in each field listed in the Create or edit data in record area.

7. After you finish entering information in a field, advance to the next field by pressing Tab or clicking Next Field. If you want to edit a previous field, press Shift+Tab or click Previous Field.

8. After you finish entering the information for the last field, press Enter or click New Record.

This step adds the information for the first record to the new data table and clears all the fields in the "Quick Data Entry" dialog box for your next record entry.

9. Repeat Steps 6 through 8 to continue adding records to the new data file. After you finish adding your last record, click Close to close the "Quick Data Entry" dialog box.

WordPerfect 9 displays an alert box that asks whether you want to save the changes to disk.

10. Click Yes to save the document that contains the new data file.

If you prefer to wait and save the document after you have a chance to check over the data table, click No instead.

11. Enter the new filename in the "Save Data File" dialog box and click OK.

Creating a form file

After you create a data file with the data records, you have to create a form file, which indicates how and where each piece of information (field) from the data file is used. The form file contains both boilerplate text and field codes that say, in effect, "Put this piece of information from each record right here." To create a form file, follow these steps:

1. Choose Tools⇨Merge or press Shift+F9 to open the "Merge" dialog box.

2. Choose Create Document to begin creating the form file.

If the current document is not empty, the "Create Merge File" dialog box appears with the "New document window" radio button selected.

3. Click OK or press Enter to create the data file in the current document window, or click the "New document window" radio button to create the data file in a new document window before you click OK or press Enter.

WordPerfect 9 then opens the "Associate Form and Data" dialog box, which is where you indicate the data file you're using for the merge with the new form file.

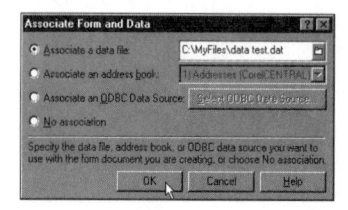

4. Type the filename of the data file in the "Associate a data file" text box or select it with the list-file button to the right of the text box.

If you don't know which data file you want to use with the form file you're creating, choose the "No association" radio button.

5. Click OK or press Enter.

WordPerfect 9 then closes the "Create Form File" dialog box and returns you to a new (or current) document window. At the same time, the program displays the Merge Property Bar.

6. Insert FIELD merge codes at each place in the form file where you want WordPerfect 9 to merge information from the records in the data file:

   a. Choose Merge Codes on the Merge Property Bar.

   The "Insert Merge Codes" dialog box opens.

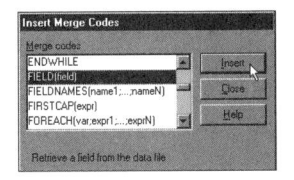

   b. Select FIELD(field) in the "Merge codes" list box and then click Insert to open the "Insert Field Name or Number" dialog box.

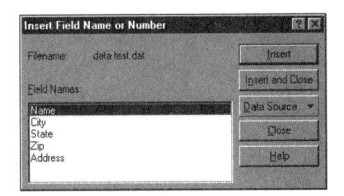

   Be sure to include all necessary punctuation and spaces between FIELD codes.

Merge

  c. Type the field name or, if you've associated a data file, choose an existing field name from the data file and press Enter or click Insert.

  d. Repeat this procedure for each field you want merged from the data file.

  Every time you perform this procedure, WordPerfect 9 inserts the FIELD merge code with the name of the field you selected. If you selected the Company field, for example, you see FIELD(Company) in the text.

7. After you're finished composing the form document by combining the canned text with the appropriate field names, click Insert and Close to close the "Insert Field Name or Number" dialog box; then click Close to close the "Insert Merge Codes" dialog box to return to your new form file.

8. Save the file by using Save or Save As from the File menu (or by pressing Ctrl+S).

> **TIP:** To insert the current date in the text of the form letter, choose DATE in the "Merge codes" list box of the "Insert Merge Codes" dialog box before clicking Insert. WordPerfect 9 then inserts the DATE merge code at the insertion point's current position.

Merging the data and form file

After you have created your data and form files, you're ready to rock 'n' roll (well, at least to perform the merge). To perform the standard merge, follow these steps:

1. Choose File⇨Open and open the form file you want to use in the merge.

2. Open the "Merge" dialog box by clicking Merge on the Merge Property Bar, by choosing Tools⇨Merge, or by pressing Shift+F9.

3. Click Merge in the "Merge" dialog box to open the "Perform Merge" dialog box.

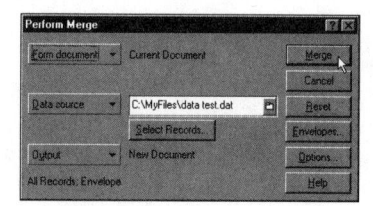

    4. Select a form document, data source, and output file description using the drop-down lists in the "Perform Merge" dialog box.

    5. Change any of these settings as necessary by selecting the appropriate text box. Then enter the filename or select it with the list-file button located to the right of each text box.

    6. Click Merge or press Enter to begin the merge.

        The program merges information from records in the data file with copies of the form file, creating a new merged form for each record used. WordPerfect 9 keeps you informed by showing its progress on the Status bar.

Envelopes and labels

Keep in mind that you can have WordPerfect 9 generate an envelope for each form letter you create in the merge. To do so, click Envelopes in the "Perform Merge" dialog box. Then fill out the information in the envelope that appears in the document window. Use the Insert Field button to copy the appropriate FIELD codes from the data file into the Mailing Addresses area of the Envelope. WordPerfect 9 then generates an envelope for each record during the merge and places all the envelopes after the form letters that are produced (see the "Envelope" section earlier in this part).

To create mailing labels for your form letters, you have to create a form file that you insert into just the first label. This file uses a label form with the appropriate FIELD codes for the associated data file. Then you perform a merge by using this label form file and the data file whose fields are referred to (see the "Labels" section earlier in this part for more information).

For more information about this command, see Chapter 17 of *WordPerfect 9 For Windows For Dummies*.

Page Size

This feature lets you choose a new paper size for all pages or particular pages in your document.

To choose just the right paper size for your print job, follow these steps:

    1. Choose File➪Page Setup to open the "Page Setup" dialog box.

Page Size

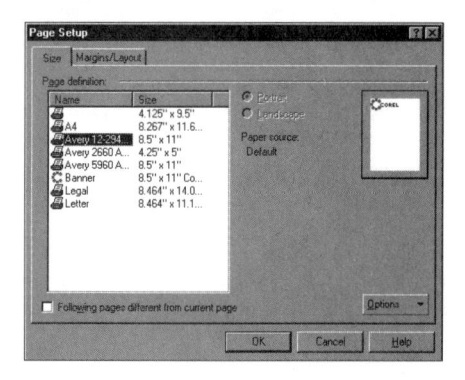

2. Choose from the following options on the Size tab of the "Page Setup" dialog box:

   - **Page definition:** Lets you choose the style of paper you want to use from a number of default sizes. Custom page sizes are also added to this list as you create them. Choose Portrait or Landscape view for your page using the appropriate radio buttons.

   On the Options drop-down menu:

   - **Edit:** Lets you edit the paper definition that's highlighted in the "Edit Page Size" dialog box.

   - **Delete:** Lets you delete the paper definition that's highlighted in the "Page information" list box.

   - **New:** Lets you create a new paper definition for your printer in the "New Page Size" dialog box.

   - **Regenerate:** Lets you restore previously deleted page definitions for the current printer driver and add new definitions that may have been created on the system since the last time the list was generated.

3. After you're finished selecting a page size, click OK or press Enter to return to the open document.

> **TIP:** If you want the subsequent pages in your document to use a different page size, click the "Following pages different from current page" check box to display this version of the Size tab of the "Page Setup" dialog box:

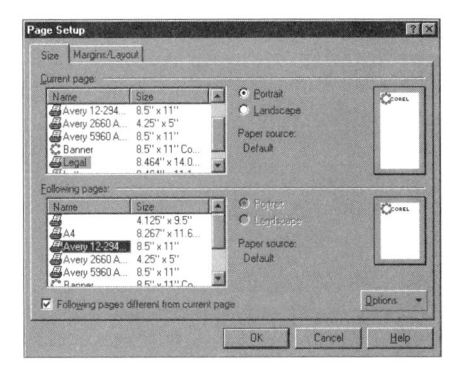

Print

This command prints all or part of the document located in the current document editing window.

You want print features? WordPerfect 9 has print features. Follow these steps to see them all:

1. Choose File➪Print or press Ctrl+P to open the "Print to [Your Printer]" dialog box.

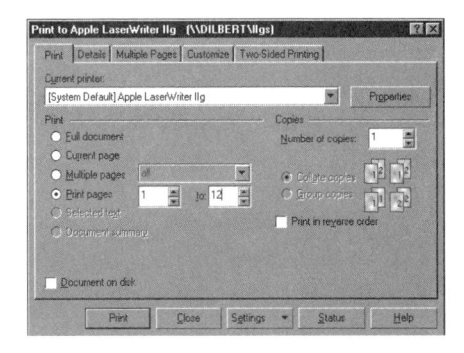

2. Make a selection from the following options in the "Print to [Your Printer]" dialog box.

On the Print tab:

- **Current printer:** Lets you use the drop-down list to select a new printer to use (a printer you installed with Windows or a WordPerfect printer you installed when you installed the program).

- **Properties:** Displays the "Properties" dialog box for the current printer. You can specify settings for each printer you select.

- **Print area:** Lets you click a radio button to select which section of the document to print. You can choose Full document (the default), Current page, Print pages, Multiple pages, Selected text, or Document summary. The "Document on disk" checkbox enables you to print a document saved to a hard drive, floppy disk, or networked drive.

- **Copies area:** Lets you specify the number of copies to print using the Number of copies text box. You can use the "Collate copies" or "Group copies" radio buttons to group or collate your documents. You can also use the "Print in reverse order" check box to print the last page of your document first.

On the Details tab:

- **Current printer area:** Lets you specify printer-specific information, add a printer, set printer properties, and select an initial font.

- **Resolution area:** Lets you change printer resolution, print in color, print text as graphics, or print text only. You can include the document summary when printing if one has been written for the document.

The other tabs on the "Print to [Your Printer]" dialog box:

- **Multiple Pages tab:** Provides options for printing specific pages or labels, secondary pages, chapters, or volumes.

- **Customize tab:** Enables you to select a percentage to enlarge or reduce the document, scale to fit the output page, and choose size dimensions to create poster or thumbnail size documents.

- **Two-Sided Printing tab:** Provides options for printing on both sides of the paper and creating booklets.

Finally, these option buttons at the bottom of the "Print to [Your Printer]" dialog box:

- **Settings:** Displays the Named settings drop-down list, where you can save named print configuration settings.

- **Status:** Displays the "Print Status and History" dialog box.

3. After you finish configuring your print job, click Print or press Enter to send the job to the printer.

Tip: When you click Print to begin a print job, WordPerfect 9 sends the print job to the print queue. If you want to cancel the printing:

1. Click <u>S</u>tatus on the "Print" dialog box to open the "Print Status and History" dialog box.

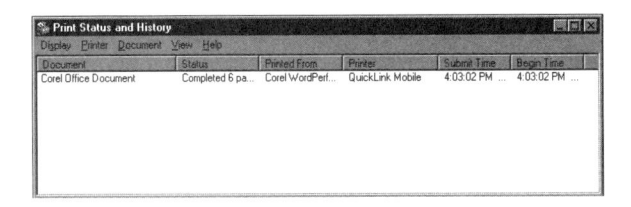

Document	Status	Printed From	Printer	Submit Time	Begin Time
Corel Office Document	Completed 6 pa...	Corel WordPerf...	QuickLink Mobile	4:03:02 PM ...	4:03:02 PM ...

2. Choose <u>D</u>ocument⇨<u>C</u>ancel Printing.

Cross-Reference: For more information about this command, see Chapter 12 of *WordPerfect 9 For Windows For Dummies*.

Making Your Work Go Faster

I'm assuming that anyone who went out and bought a quick reference in the first place will not mind a few tips on how to make work go faster. You've obviously got better things to do than spend your lunch hour pondering why it seems that computers haven't really made life easier.

In Part V, I cover all the tips and shortcuts that make WordPerfect 9 users so much nicer to take out to lunch.

In this part . . .

- ✓ Autoscroll
- ✓ Corrections on the fly
- ✓ **Property Bars: Why are they so context-sensitive?**
- ✓ **Making macros**
- ✓ **How to Go To**
- ✓ **Fast Formatting**
- ✓ **All about QuickMenus**
- ✓ **Searching with QuickFinder**

Part V

Application Bar

This bar keeps you informed of lots of useful information and can be expanded to include more utilities than Batman's belt.

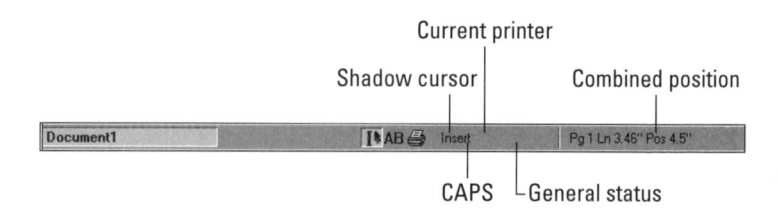

Current printer, Shadow cursor, Combined position, CAPS, General status — labeled on Application Bar figure showing: `Document1    I AB 🖨 Insert    Pg 1 Ln 3.45" Pos 4.5"`

The default Application bar shown in the preceding figure includes these features:

+ **Shadow cursor on/off:** Turns the shadow cursor on and off (see "Shadow Cursor" later in this part).

+ **CAPS:** Turns Caps Lock on and off.

+ **Current printer:** Displays the name of the current printer.

+ **General status:** Indicates Insert or Typeover mode and displays information on columns, tables, macros, merges, paragraph styles, and so on.

+ **Combined position:** Displays page number, line, and cursor position. Click this button to open the "Go To" dialog box.

You can change which information is displayed on the Application bar and how it is displayed using these steps:

1. Click the Application bar with the secondary mouse button and choose Settings on the QuickMenu.

The "Application Bar Settings" dialog box opens.

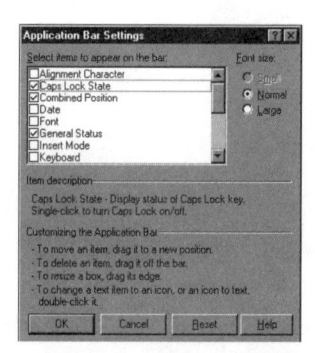

2. To add or remove items, select or deselect their check boxes in the "Select items to appear on the bar" list box.

   3. Use the Font size radio buttons to select the size for the text on the Application bar.

   4. Use the Reset button to return the Application bar to its default settings.

   5. Click OK to close the "Application Bar Settings" dialog box.

TIP

While the "Applications Bar Settings" dialog box is open, you can use drag and drop with the mouse to alter the appearance of the Application bar in the following ways:

- ✦ To rearrange the order of the items on the Application bar, click and drag their buttons to new positions.
- ✦ To delete an item, click and drag it off the Application bar.
- ✦ To resize an item, position the mouse pointer on the item's border and, when the pointer changes to a double-headed arrow, drag the border in the appropriate direction.

FAST TRACK

You can perform any of the above commands when the "Application Bar Settings" dialog box is closed by pressing the Alt key before you drag and drop.

Auto Scroll

WORDPERFECT 9 New!

Auto Scroll lets you scroll through your document quickly and without using the arrow keys or the scroll bars. Point the Auto Scroll arrow in the direction you want to move, and Auto Scroll scrolls through the document for you. The scrolling speed increases if you move the arrow further away from the Auto Scroll tool and slows if you move the arrow closer to the Auto Scroll tool.

To move through a document using Auto Scroll, follow these steps:

   1. Click the Autoscroll button on the WordPerfect 9 toolbar to change the cursor to the Autoscroll arrow.

   2. Click inside your document.

   3. Do one of the following:

   - Move the mouse to the top of the page to move upward through the document. The Autoscroll arrow points up.
   - Move the mouse to the bottom of the page to move downward through the document. The Autoscroll arrow points down.

   4. To stop Auto Scrolling, click the mouse.

> You can also stop Auto Scrolling by pressing a key.

Bookmark

Use this feature to mark a place in a document so that you can return to that location quickly.

Creating a bookmark

To create a bookmark, follow these steps:

1. Click where you want to insert a bookmark.

2. Click Tools⇨Bookmark to open the "Bookmark" dialog box.

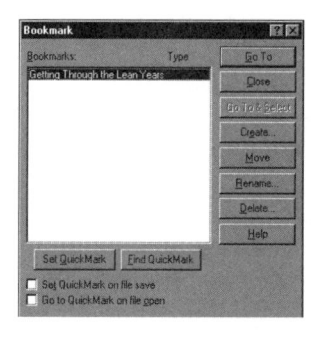

3. Choose from the following options:

- **Bookmarks:** List all bookmarks in the current document.
- **Set QuickMark:** Place a QuickMark at the insertion point in the current document.
- **Find QuickMark:** Move the insertion point to the QuickMark in the current document.
- **Set QuickMark on file save:** Place a bookmark at the insertion point whenever you save a document so that you can return to that location quickly.
- **Go to QuickMark on file open:** Move the insertion point directly to the QuickMark each time you open this file.

When you've selected from these options, you can use the following buttons:

- **Go To:** Move the insertion point to the selected bookmark.

- **Go To & Select:** Moves the insertion point to the bookmark and selects the associated text. This option is only available for bookmarks with selected text.
- **Create:** Name and insert a new bookmark at the insertion point.
- **Move:** Move the selected bookmark from its previous location to the insertion point.
- **Rename:** Rename the selected bookmark.
- **Delete:** Delete the selected bookmark.

4. Click Close to close the "Bookmark" dialog box and save all changes.

Finding a bookmark

After you create a bookmark, it's a snap to use them:

1. Click Tools⇨Bookmark.
2. Select the name of the bookmark in the "Bookmark" dialog box.
3. Click Go To.

Click Go To & Select to move the insertion point to the selected bookmark and select the text again.

Using a QuickMark

QuickMarks are great for marking a spot in the document that changes. For example, mark the place where you stop writing in a document with a QuickMark, and when you open the document later to continue writing, use the QuickMark to go right to the place you left off.

Setting a QuickMark

1. Click where you want to insert the QuickMark.
2. Click Tools⇨Bookmark.
3. Click Set QuickMark or any of the other QuickMark options in the "Bookmark" dialog box.

Finding a QuickMark

1. Click Tools⇨Bookmark.
2. Click Find QuickMark in the "Bookmark" dialog box.

To automatically go to the QuickMark when you open the document, select Go to QuickMark on file open.

DAD (Desktop Applications Director)

Use the Desktop Applications Director (DAD) to place program icons in the notification area (that area with the little icons east of the Start button) of the Windows taskbar. Then, when you want to run a program, simply click the program icon on the taskbar.

Let's add to DAD

To add program icons to the Desktop Applications Director, follow these steps:

1. Click any of the DAD program icons on the Windows taskbar with the secondary mouse button and then click Properties to open the "DAD Properties" dialog box.

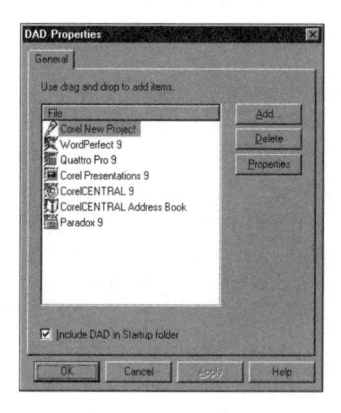

2. Click Add and then choose the executable file or shortcut you want to add to DAD.

3. Click OK to apply the changes to DAD.

> **TIP:** If you choose Properties on the "DAD Properties" dialog box and make changes to the shortcut Properties, you need to close and restart DAD before the changes take effect (see how in the next two segments).

How to get rid of DAD

1. Click any of the DAD icons on the Windows taskbar with the secondary mouse button.

2. Click Exit DAD.

How to get DAD started

1. Click Start on the Windows taskbar.

2. Choose WordPerfect Office 2000➪Utilities➪Corel Desktop Application Director 9.

TIP: QuickTips appear when you hold your mouse pointer over a DAD program icon in the notification area of the Windows taskbar. You can edit these QuickTips and, at the same time, change the name of the application on the DAD menu with these steps:

1. Click any of the DAD program icons in the notification area of the Windows taskbar with the secondary mouse button and then click Properties to open the "DAD Properties" dialog box.

2. Click to select the application you want to change, pause, and then click the name again.

The name is placed in a small editing box.

3. Type a new QuickTip and then press Enter.

Date/Time

This tool puts today's date in your document as text, which you must update yourself, or as a secret code, which WordPerfect 9 updates every time you open the document.

Inserting the date as text

To insert the current date as text, which doesn't change unless you open the document and edit it, follow these steps:

1. Position the insertion point where you want the date to appear.

2. Choose Insert➪Date/Time to open the "Date/Time" dialog box.

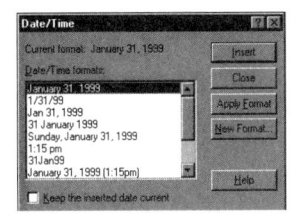

3. Select from the following options:

- **Date/Time formats:** Select a date/time format from the scroll list.
- **Apply Format:** Apply the date/time format selected in the Date/Time formats scroll list.
- **New Format:** Create a new date/time format and add it to the list.
- **Insert:** Save the date/time format in the document and close the dialog box.

Inserting the date as a secret code

To insert the date as a secret code, which WordPerfect 9 automatically keeps up-to-date for you, follow these steps:

1. Position the insertion point where you want the date to appear.
2. Choose Insert⇨Date/Time to open the "Date/Time" dialog box.
3. Select a Date/Time format.
4. Click to place a check mark in the "Keep the inserted date current" check box.
5. Click Insert to save the date and return to the open document.

FAST TRACK You can quickly insert an automatically updating date/time in your document by positioning the insertion point where you want the date to appear and pressing Ctrl+Shift+D.

Dragon NaturallySpeaking

Corel's Office 2000 Suite includes really cool voice recognition software called Dragon NaturallySpeaking . You can use this software to dictate text directly into a WordPerfect document and use voice commands to navigate and format the document text.

After installing and training the program to recognize your voice, the Dragon NaturallySpeaking pull-down menu appears to the right of Help on the WordPerfect 9 menu bar each time you launch WordPerfect 9. Note that if you haven't finished training the program to understand your particular voice patterns (part of the installation of NaturallySpeaking), you will be prompted to do so before you can start using its features.

Dragon NaturallySpeaking

In addition, a new button, Use NaturalWord, is added to the right side of the WordPerfect 9 toolbar. Clicking this button launches the program and displays four other buttons in this area of the toolbar, as shown in the following table.

Icon	Button Name	Function
	Use NaturalWord	Click this button to Start Dragon NaturallySpeaking software.
	Save User File	Saves your current user files. Use this feature after you modify or add new words to NaturallySpeaking, so that your changes are there for you the next time you start your user file.
	Train a Word or Phrase	Lets you train NaturallySpeaking to learn new words and phrases that it hasn't encountered yet. You should train NaturallySpeaking to learn any words that it doesn't know. After it knows the word, you can dictate it to your computer.
	Search for New Words	Finds all the words in the current document that NaturallySpeaking doesn't know.
	Turn Microphone On/Off	Lets you turn the NaturallySpeaking Microphone on or off. When you want your computer to start or stop listening to what you say, use this toggle button.

Take this down

To start dictating text in a WordPerfect document, follow these steps.

1. If the program is not already running, choose Dragon NaturallySpeaking⇨Use NaturalWord on the WordPerfect menu bar, or click the Use NaturalWord button on the WordPerfect toolbar.

2. Click the Turn On the microphone button on the WordPerfect 9 toolbar. The computer is now listening to your every word. (Remember to have a microphone hooked up to your computer.)

3. Begin speaking. As you speak, your computer will start translating your speech into text.

4. Remember to speak clearly. Voice Recognition has come a long way, but it isn't quite human yet.

A word to the wise

Your computer only knows words that it's heard before, so you must train NaturallySpeaking to recognize what you say. To train new words or phrases, do the following:

1. If the program is not already running, choose Dragon NaturallySpeaking▷Use NaturalWord on the WordPerfect menu bar, or click the Use NaturalWord button on the WordPerfect toolbar.

2. Click the Train New Word or Phrase button on the WordPerfect 9 toolbar.

3. Type or paste the new vocabulary that you want the program to recognize in the Enter the word or phrase you want to train text box, then click OK.

4. Click the Record button, and speak the word or phrase that appears in the Please say text box.

5. When you're finished, click Done.

New words in the document

The best way to add words to NaturallySpeaking's vocabulary, thereby making it "smarter" and more useful, is to add words that occur in your own documents. To do this, follow these steps:

1. If the program is not already running, choose Dragon NaturallySpeaking▷Use NaturalWord on the WordPerfect menu bar, or click the Use NaturalWord button on the WordPerfect toolbar.

2. Open a document that has words you want to add to NaturallySpeaking's vocabulary (or use the document that's currently open).

3. Click the Find New Words button in the toolbar. The "Find New Words" dialog box appears with an alphabetical list of new words.

4. You can select individual words by clicking on the check box next to a word, or you can click Select All to select all the words.

TIP: Words that are not proper nouns but appear capitalized in the document (as they are when they begin a sentence) will show up in this list. To exclude these words from the Training list, select the "Hide existing vocabulary words with different capitalization" check box. What's left is just the words that are truly "new."

1. Click Train to start teaching NaturallySpeaking your chosen list of words.

2. Click the Record button, and speak the word or phrase that appears in the Please say text box.

3. NaturallySpeaking records the word, then automatically displays the next word from your list. Continue saying the words as they appear in the Please say text box.

4. When you're finished, click Done.

Show me what you know

Besides understanding what you say, NaturallySpeaking also follows your commands (unlike your boss). You can voice many commands to your computer when the microphone is on. For a complete list of commands that NaturallySpeaking knows, choose Dragon NaturallySpeaking⇨Help.

Here are some of the categories of basic editing commands that NaturallySpeaking has been taught to listen for:

- **Selecting:** To highlight text and make changes to it (just as you would by clicking and dragging with a mouse). To select any word, say the word "Select" followed by the word you want selected. To select a phrase such as "with five dozen milk jugs" from a sentence, you say, "Select *with* through *jugs*."

- **Formatting**: To change the formatting of selected words or paragraphs, you can say, "Underline that," "Bold that," "Italicize that," and "Restore that" (removes formatting). Also, you can change the current Font by saying, "Set font, Times," "Format that 12 point," and "Times New Roman 24 bold."

- **Deleting**: To delete text, say "Select" followed by the word you want deleted. For a range of words, say "Select Dear John through Goodbye Forever" and then say, "Delete that." You can also select text and say "Delete next word," or "Delete previous 4 words."

- **Navigating**: You can move to the top or bottom of a document or the beginning or end of a line by saying: "Go to top," "Move to start of line," "Move to end of line," or "Move to end of document."

In addition, NaturallySpeaking has included the most common commands to keep your fingers from forever touching the mouse and keyboard:

- To Undo your last action, say, "Undo that."
- To capitalize text, say, "Cap that," "All cap that," or "No caps that."
- To punctuate a sentence with a period, say, "Period."
- To start a new paragraph, say, "New paragraph."

Go To

This command moves the insertion point to a specific place in the document, such as its last position in the text or the top of a particular page.

You can choose to move the insertion point to its last known position, to the top or bottom of the current page, or to a particular page number or bookmark. Here's how:

   1. Choose Edit⇨Go To or press Ctrl+G to open the "Go To" dialog box.

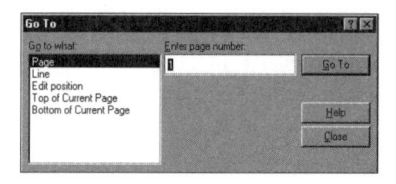

   2. Use these options to define where you want to go:

   - **Go to what:** Move the insertion point to a particular position — Page, Line, Edit position, Top of Current Page, or Bottom of Current Page.

   - **Enter page number:** Move the insertion point to the beginning of a particular page entered or chosen from the scroll list.

   3. Click Go To or press Enter to close the "Go To" dialog box.

Grammar-As-You-Go

(See "Proofread" later in this part.)

Hide Bars

This command removes all the bars from the screen, including the title bar, menu bar, Property bar, WordPerfect 9 toolbar, Ruler bar, scroll bars, and Status bar. You see only the document text and graphics.

To give your screen that wide-open-spaces look:

   1. Choose View⇨Hide Bars or press Alt+Shift+F5 to open the "Hide Bars Information" dialog box.

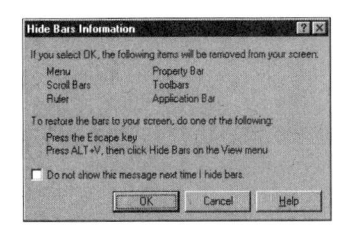

When you choose this command, WordPerfect 9 displays the "Hide Bars Information" dialog box. This box lets you know that you're about to hide all the bars in the WordPerfect 9 program and document windows (including the all-important menu bar). The box also tells you how to bring the bars back.

2. To get rid of the bars, choose OK or press Enter.

> **TIP**
> If you don't want to be bothered with the display of the "Hide Bar Information" dialog box, click the "Do not show this message next time I hide bars" option to put a check mark in its check box.

Macros

This series of commands are key combinations that WordPerfect 9 can play back later at a much faster rate than you can possibly do manually.

Recording macros

Recording macros in WordPerfect 9 resembles the way you record cassette tapes or videotapes. After you turn on the macro recorder, WordPerfect 9 records the result of each action you perform, whether you type text or choose new format settings.

You can use the macro recorder to record several types of series. WordPerfect 9 can record a straight series of commands, such as changing the top margin to two inches and the line spacing to double spacing. It can record a straight series of words or phrases, such as Abercrombie, Fitch, Abercrombie, and Phelps. Or the program can record a combination of text and commands, such as entering the company name Baggins and Bilbo, Inc., and then centering and boldfacing this text before inserting two blank lines.

To record a macro, follow these steps:

1. Position the insertion point at a place in your document where it's safe (and possible) to execute all the WordPerfect 9 commands you want to record in your macro.

2. Choose Tools⇨Macro⇨Record or simply press Ctrl+F10 to open the "Record Macro" dialog box.

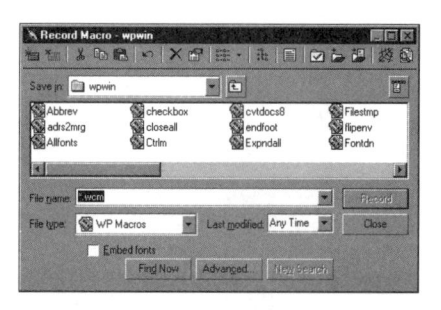

3. Enter a name for your macro in the File name text box.

    WordPerfect 9 saves your macro under this filename with the .wcm extension after you finish recording the macro.

    If the filename you specified for the macro already exists, WordPerfect 9 displays an alert box that asks whether you want to replace the existing macro. Click Yes to replace the existing macro with the one you are about to create. Click No if you want to save the macro under a different name.

4. Click Record or press Enter to begin recording the macro.

    WordPerfect 9 closes the "Record Macro" dialog box, changes the mouse pointer to the international "Don't" symbol (a circle with a line through it) to remind you that mouse moves don't work when you record a macro in WordPerfect 9, and displays the Macro toolbar.

5. Enter the text and select the commands you want to include in your macro.

    Make sure to select them in the sequence in which you want to record them. If you want to move the insertion point or select text, you must use the keyboard. (When you're recording a macro, you can use the mouse only to choose menu commands and make selections in dialog boxes.)

6. After you're finished choosing the WordPerfect 9 commands and entering the text for the macro, click the Stop macro button on the Macro toolbar to stop the recording.

Playing back macros

To play back a macro with a regular filename:

1. Choose Tools⇨Macro⇨Play or simply press Alt+F10 to open the "Play Macro" dialog box.

2. Type the macro's filename (without its .wcm extension) in the dialog box that appears.

3. Press Enter or click OK.

When you play back a macro, WordPerfect 9 plays back each command in the sequence in which it was recorded.

You can give a macro a CTRLx or CTRLSFTx name, where *x* is the mnemonic key you assign to the macro. To play back a macro so named, simply press Ctrl and the letter key or press Ctrl+Shift and the letter key. For example, if you create a macro to insert the date, name it CTRLd in the "Macro Record" dialog box. When you want to insert a date, just press the keyboard shortcut Ctrl+d to run the macro.

If your macro is not behaving as expected, you can stop the playback by pressing Esc. Because of the potential danger in playing back an untested macro, always make sure to save the current document before you play back a macro for the first time. Then, if the macro wreaks havoc in your document before you can shut it down with Esc, you can always close the trashed document without saving your changes and then open the version you saved before performing the macro.

Attaching your macro to the document template

When you choose Tools⇨Macro⇨Record, WordPerfect 9 saves the new macro in its own file. To attach the new macro to the current template (see "New (Document)" in Part II for details), follow these steps:

1. Choose Tools⇨Template Macro⇨Record to display the "Record Template Macro" dialog box.

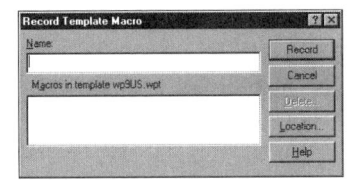

2. Enter the new macro's name in its Name text box.

   By default, WordPerfect 9 attaches the macro to whichever template is currently assigned to your document (making this macro available to any document using the same template).

   3. If you want your new macro attached to the default template, click Location and then select the Default Template radio button in the "Macro Location" dialog box.

   4. Click OK to close the "Macro Location" dialog box.

   5. After naming your macro in the "Record Template Macro" dialog box, click Record and then record your macro as you would record one saved in its own file.

WARNING

You can only use the mouse as you record the macro to choose the WordPerfect 9 commands from the menu bar and in the dialog boxes you want to include. WordPerfect 9 cannot record movements of the insertion point in the text that you make by clicking the mouse or using the scroll bars. If you want to record insertion-point movements as part of the macro, you must abandon the mouse and switch to the insertion point movement shortcut keys. (See the "Insertion Point" section in Part II for specific keystrokes.)

Prompt-As-You-Go

(See "Proofread" later in this part.)

Proofread

If you ever thought that having a nit-picking English teacher perched on your shoulder would be nice to help check your spelling and grammar while you type, then the Proofread menu commands were made for you. The Prompt-As-You-Go feature displays suggestions while you type. To be prompted as you go, do the following:

   1. Choose Tools➪Proofread➪Prompt-As-You-Go.

   When you activate Prompt-As-You-Go, a drop-down list appears on the Property bar:

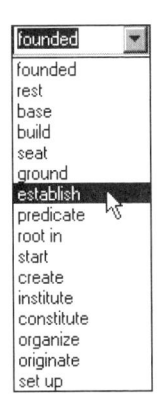

```
founded      ▼
founded
rest
base
build
seat
ground
establish
predicate
root in
start
create
institute
constitute
organize
originate
set up
```

Prompt-As-You-Go can act as a spell checker, a grammar checker, or a thesaurus, depending on where the insertion point is placed. If the insertion point is placed on a misspelled word or a possible grammar error, clicking the arrow on the Prompt-As-You-Go drop-down list displays a list of corrections. If the insertion point is placed on a word that is free of spelling or grammar errors, Prompt-As-You-Go lists possible synonyms from the thesaurus.

Prompt-As-You-Go displays possible grammar errors in blue, spelling errors in red, and thesaurus terms in black. If the box is blank, it has no suggestions for the word.

2. Click a word or marked phrase in your document.

3. Click the arrow on the Prompt-As-You-Go drop-down list on the Property bar and then select replacement text.

4. To turn off Prompt-As-You-Go, choose Tools⇨Proofread⇨Prompt-As-You-Go to remove the check mark from the menu command.

The Proofread menu also contains these options:

- ✦ **Spell-As-You-Go:** Marks words as you type that are not included in any of the Corel WordPerfect dictionaries. You can make corrections in the Prompt-As-You-Go drop-down list.

- ✦ **Grammar-As-You-Go:** Marks words or phrases that may indicate incorrect grammar or usage.

When a word is marked by Prompt-As-You-Go (red for spelling or blue for grammar), use the QuickMenu to make the correction quickly:

1. Click the marked word or phrase with the secondary mouse button to open the QuickMenu.

2. Choose from these options on the QuickMenu:

- Select the word or phrase that corrects the problem.
- Skip in <u>D</u>ocument: To use the word in the current document only.
- <u>A</u>dd: If you frequently use the word, to add it to the WordPerfect dictionaries.
- Grammatik: To use additional grammar checking options.
- Spe<u>l</u>l Checker: To start the spell checker.

Property Bar

The Property bar holds buttons that you point and click all day to do common things, such as open, save, or print a document. Because it is context-sensitive, the Property bar displays buttons and options related to the task you are performing. For example, when text is selected, the Text Property Bar appears on the Property bar containing only text-related commands. Like any other toolbar in WordPerfect 9, the Property bar can be moved, docked, or hidden away from its default position above the document window.

The buttons on the Property bar

By default, the Property bar contains the following buttons listed left to right (they're explained in the following table):

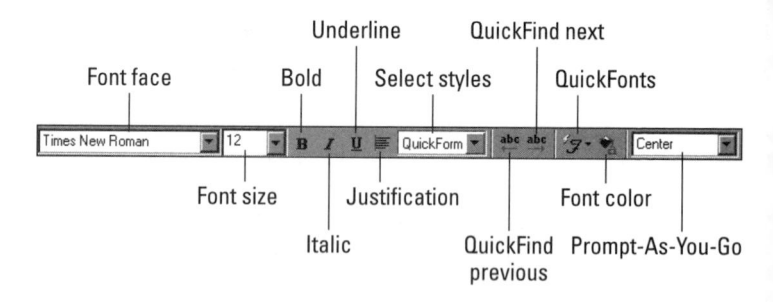

Callouts on the Property bar image:
- Font face
- Font size
- Bold
- Italic
- Underline
- Justification
- Select styles
- QuickFind previous
- QuickFind next
- QuickFonts
- Font color
- Prompt-As-You-Go

Button	Function
Font face	Change the font used in the document text (this button shows the current font).
Font size	Change the size of the font used in the document text (this button shows the current font size).

Property Bar

Button	Function
Bold, Italic, Underline	Apply or remove these font attributes to the selected text.
Justification	Change the justification of the text in the document. See "Justification" in Part III for more on changing the text alignment.
Select styles	Select a style for your document (this button shows the name of the current style or <None> when none is selected).
QuickFind previous	Find the previous occurrence of the current word or selection.
QuickFind next	Find the next occurrence of the current word or selection.
QuickFonts	Select a recently used font and font attributes.
Font color	Change the font color.
Prompt-As-You-Go	Display suggestions for proper spelling, grammar usage, and thesaurus usage. See the "Proofread" section earlier in this part for more details.

> **TIP:** Choose Hide Property Bar from the QuickMenu when you want the Property Bar to go away.

Featuring the Property bar

When you begin performing a particular task in WordPerfect 9 (such as inserting a table or merging a data file and a form file), different feature buttons appear that you mouse maniacs can use to do things related to the task at hand. As new feature buttons appear, they replace some of the default buttons on the Property bar. The figure below shows the Table Property Bar that appears on the Property bar after you insert a table into your document.

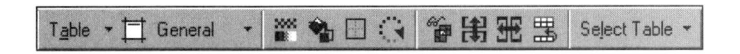

To use new feature buttons as they appear on the Property bar, simply click the button with the primary mouse button. You can also use the keyboard shortcut Alt+Shift+ the underlined letter (hot key) if the feature bar button has one.

Creating a full-length feature

Property bars are context-sensitive, meaning that only buttons related to the task at hand appear. Although you can't change the context of the buttons, you can choose which of the available buttons in that context appear on the feature bar. To edit the Property bar and its ever changing features, follow these steps:

Property Bar

1. Click the Property bar with the secondary mouse button and choose Edit to open the "Property Bar Editor" dialog box.

In this example, I clicked the Table feature bar with the secondary mouse button.

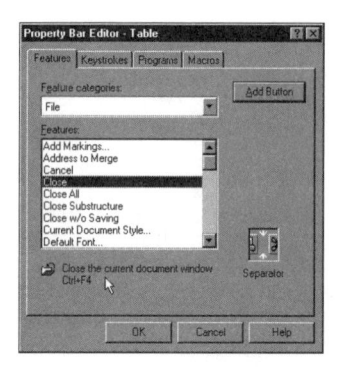

2. Select from the following options on the Features tab:

- **Feature categories:** Use the drop-down list to choose which type of related features you want to add to the Property bar.
- **Features:** Choose the features you want to add from the scroll list. When you select a feature, a description appears in the lower-left corner of the dialog box.
- **Add Button:** Add the selected feature to the Property bar.
- **Separator:** Add a separator between buttons so that you can group similar buttons together. Drag to the toolbar or Property bar you are editing and drop where you want to add a separator.

3. Click the following tabs to select their options:

- **Keystrokes tab:** Add a Property bar button that types the keystrokes you specify.
- **Programs tab:** Add a program to the Property bar.
- **Macros tab:** Add a macro to a Property bar button.

4. Click OK or press Enter after you're through editing the toolbar.

TIP

When you click an item in the Features drop-down list of the "Property Bar Editor" dialog box, the arrow pointer displays an icon for that button. Double-click the item to add that feature to the toolbar.

QuickCorrect

This command lets you designate the typos that you routinely make and tell WordPerfect which corrections it should automatically undertake the moment your erring fingers make these boo-boos.

To set up the QuickCorrect function, follow these steps:

1. Choose Tools⇨QuickCorrect to open the "QuickCorrect" dialog box:

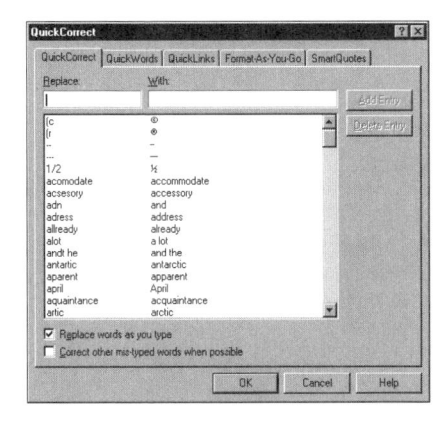

2. Use these options on the QuickCorrect tab:

- **Replace:** Type the incorrect spelling that you invariably enter in your document in this text box.

- **With:** Type the correct (make sure that it's correct) spelling that you want WordPerfect to use whenever you type the incorrect spelling you just entered in the Replace text box.

- **Add Entry:** Click this button to add your new QuickCorrect entry to the list.

- **Delete Entry:** Click this button to remove the selected QuickCorrect entry from its list box.

- **Replace words as you type:** Keep this check box checked if you want WordPerfect to make corrections as soon as you make the typo. If you deselect this check box, the program does not make your corrections until you spell check the part of the document containing the error (see "Spell Checker" in Part II for details on spell checking a document).

- **Correct other mistyped words when possible:** If this option is selected, mistyped words that have only one possible correction are automatically replaced. Use this option only if you are confident that your document uses words found in the standard word list. Unusual spellings and proper nouns may be changed automatically.

QuickFinder

WordPerfect greatly enhanced its QuickFinder feature in WordPerfect 9. QuickFinder now consists of two components: QuickFinder Searcher and QuickFinder Manager.

QuickFinder Searcher

The QuickFinder Searcher is directly available in file management (Open, Save, and Save As), dialog boxes. QuickFinder is used to quickly find files that meet the criteria you specify. See the "Open (Document)," "Save," and "Save As" sections in Part II to review these dialog boxes. To use QuickFinder Searcher in a file management dialog box, follow these steps:

1. Click the Goto/From Search Results for Quick Finder button on the file management dialog box you are currently using (Open, Save, or Save As).

   The following figure shows the QuickFinder "Search Results" dialog box accessed from the "Open File" dialog box. Use the Goto/From Search Results for QuickFinder button to toggle between the QuickFinder "Search Results" dialog box and the current file management dialog box. By the way, this button gets my nomination for "Longest Button Title this side of Redmond." Feel free to email me the titles of any other contenders.

   Go to/From Search Results for QuickFinder button

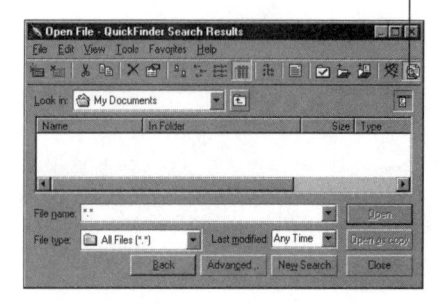

2. Specify the drive or folder you want to search in the Look in drop-down list.
3. Type a name such as **myfile** in the File name text box.
4. Select a file type such as ***.wpd** for WordPerfect documents in the File type text box.
5. Select criterion from the Last modified drop-down list.
6. Click Find now to start QuickFinder.

   QuickFinder locates the files whose title or contents meet the search criteria you specify and displays them in the QuickFinder Search Results folder, along with their locations. You can change the view and manipulate the files just as you can files in any file management dialog box.

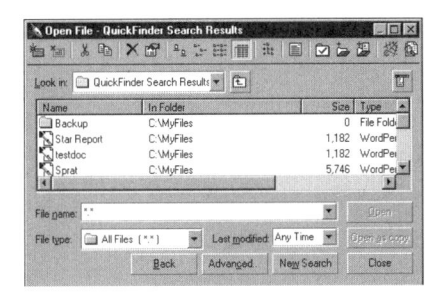

7. Click Back to return to the regular file management dialog box, or click the New Search button to start a new search.

Click the Stop Find button at any time during a search to stop the search.

TIP: QuickFinder searches can be as simple as specifying a filename to find or as sophisticated as finding all .wpd files created during the last week containing a specific word.

QuickFinder can also perform Fast Searches, which require that you specify folders, drives, or both. Then, instead of searching each individual file, QuickFinder creates a full-text, alphabetical list of every word contained in the files and folders you specified and uses this Fast Search file to find what you need. This type of search is useful when you search often, when your search criteria is complex, or when you are searching across multiple folders and drives.

QuickFinder

If you feel the need to start searching for things on your computer the second your desktop appears upon booting up, you can quickly access QuickFinder Searcher by clicking the Start button on the Task Bar to open the Start menu and choose WordPerfect Office 2000➪Utilities➪Corel QuickFinder 9 Searcher.

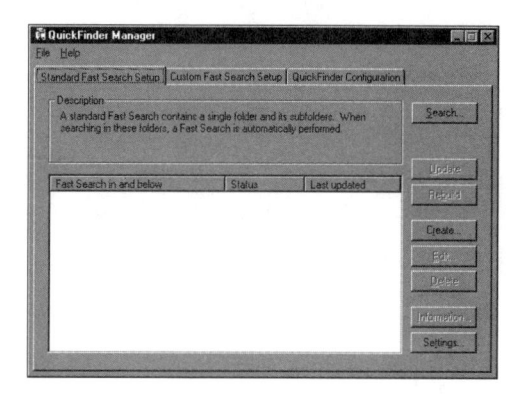

QuickFinder Manager

QuickFinder Manager is used to create, edit, and manage Fast Search files. When you use QuickFinder Manager to create a Fast Search, you group together folders and subfolders you search in often. Think of QuickFinder Manager as a "database" of often-searched folders and subfolders. When you perform a search on those folders or subfolders, QuickFinder uses the corresponding Fast Search file containing an alphabetical list of every word in the searched files. Once a Fast Search file is created, you can use it for subsequent searches of the same folders and subfolders. Searching a Fast Search file is much quicker than searching each individual file.

To access QuickFinder Manager, click the Start button on the Task Bar to open the Start menu and choose WordPerfect Office 2000➪Utilities➪Corel QuickFinder 9 Searcher.

Select from the following options on the "QuickFinder Manager" dialog box:

- ✦ **Standard Fast Search Setup:** View standard Fast Searches that contain a single folder and its subfolders.

- ✦ **Custom Fast Search Setup:** View custom Fast Searches that can contain multiple folders with or without their subfolders. Custom searches are accessed when you click the Advanced button on file management dialog boxes.

✦ **QuickFinder Configuration:** Determine where access to QuickFinder appears on your menus and enable/disable QuickFinder's automatic index updating feature.

> **TIP:** Besides creating, editing, deleting, or updating a Fast Search, keep in mind that you can also perform searches from QuickFinder Manager.

QuickFormat

This tool copies the formatting used in the current paragraph and then allows you to apply this formatting to other selections of text in the document.

To use the QuickFormat feature:

1. Position the insertion point in the paragraph whose formatting you want to use elsewhere in the document.

2. Choose Format➪QuickFormat, or click anywhere in the text with the secondary mouse button and choose QuickFormat from the QuickMenu to open the "QuickFormat" dialog box:

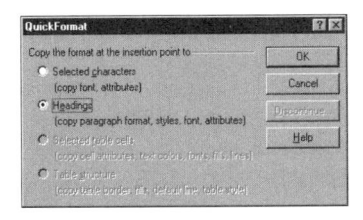

3. Choose from the following options:

    - **Selected characters:** Copies the format of text at the insertion point so that you can apply the format to other text.

    - **Headings:** Copies the format of the heading at the insertion point so that you can apply the format to other headings.

    - **Selected table cells:** Copies the format of table cells you have selected so that you can apply the format to other table cells.

    - **Table structure:** Copies the format of the current table so that you can apply the format to other tables.

    - **Discontinue:** Stops automatically updating headings that use the same QuickFormat style.

4. Choose OK or press Enter to close the "QuickFormat" dialog box.

130 QuickMark

The mouse pointer changes to a paint roller. Use this roller to select all the text you want formatted with the fonts, attributes, and styles found in the original paragraph. As soon as you release the mouse button after selecting the text, the text takes on the font, attribute, and paragraph style formatting used in the original selected paragraph.

When you no longer want to use the pointer to QuickFormat text, click in the document with the secondary mouse button and choose QuickFormat from the QuickMenu.

QuickMark

(See "Bookmark" earlier in this part.)

QuickMenu

This option lets you select commands from a limited menu that appears when you click an object (such as text or a graphics box) with the secondary mouse button.

In WordPerfect 9, you can find QuickMenus attached to each of the following screen objects:

+ Left margin area of the document (see the section "Select (Text)" in Part II)
+ Top and bottom area of the document (see the section "Header/Footer" in Part II)
+ Menu bar
+ Toolbar (see the "Toolbars" section later in this part)
+ Property bar (see the "Property Bar" section earlier in this part)
+ Scroll bars
+ Status bar
+ Document area and document text
+ Graphics boxes
+ Table cells

QuickWords

This tool lets you define an abbreviation for stock text you use and then use that abbreviation to enter the stock text into the document.

Creating QuickWords

To create QuickWords, follow these steps:

1. Type the text you want to assign a QuickWord to and then select (highlight) the text.

2. Choose Tools⇨QuickWords to open the QuickWords tab on the "QuickCorrect" dialog box.

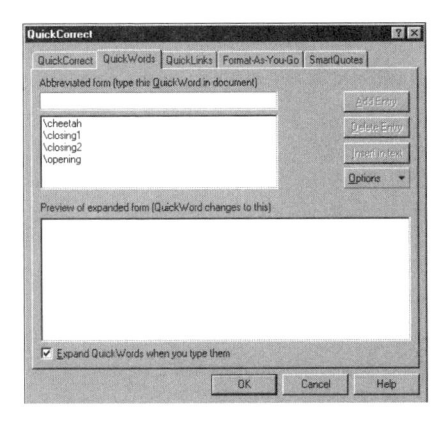

3. Select the options for the QuickWord from the following choices:

    - **Abbreviated form (type this QuickWord in document):** Designates the QuickWord that you type to insert the associated text in the document.

    - **Preview of expanded form (QuickWord changes to this):** Shows what the QuickWord looks like after it is expanded in the document.

    - **Add Entry:** Adds a QuickWord to the list.

    - **Delete Entry:** Removes a QuickWord from the list.

    - **Insert in text:** Inserts the text represented by the QuickWord in your document.

    - **Options:** Allows you to select options for formatting expanded text and renaming QuickWord entries.

4. Type the QuickWord you want to assign to the selected text in the Abbreviated form text box.

5. Click OK or press Enter to close the "QuickCorrect" dialog box.

Using QuickWords

After you create an abbreviation, you can use it to type a longer word or phrase. Here's how:

1. Type the QuickWord in the document.

2. Press Enter, Tab, or spacebar to expand it.

> **TIP:** QuickWords less than three words long can be expanded automatically as you type. To use this feature, make sure to put a check mark in the "Expand QuickWords" checkbox when you type them in the "QuickWords" dialog box.

Repeat

This feature repeats a keystroke or action, such as moving the insertion point or deleting a character, a set number of times.

Repeat is one of those WordPerfect 9 features that seems really neat when you first hear about it, but is too often overlooked when you're actually editing. WordPerfect 9 originally added this feature to allow you to easily insert a string of characters into your document, such as ——— or ********.

To repeat a character, follow these steps:

1. Choose Edit⇨Repeat Next Action to open the "Repeat" dialog box.

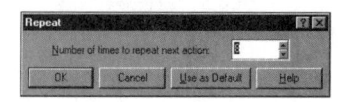

2. In the Number of times to repeat next action scroll list, enter the number desired by typing in the text box or using the scroll list buttons.

3. Choose OK or press Enter to close the "Repeat" dialog box.

4. Then type the single character or perform the action you want to repeat.

> **TIP:** You can use the Repeat feature to repeat certain keystrokes and to type characters, for example:
>
> ✦ Delete the next eight characters from the insertion point by pressing Delete.

- Move the insertion point in your document eight characters to the right by pressing the → key.
- Move eight pages up in the document by pressing PgUp.

Shadow Cursor (The Shadow [Cursor] Knows)

As you work in a document, the insertion point changes to a shadow cursor when you point to text or to white space. Where the shadow cursor goes, the insertion point follows when you click the mouse.

Using the shadow cursor

Here are some cool things the shadow cursor can do:

- When the shadow cursor appears in the white space of your document, click anywhere to start typing text.
- Drag to insert clip art, a text box, or a table.
- The shadow cursor changes appearance to show how text will be aligned when you start typing.

TIP You no longer need to insert blank lines manually to leave space between paragraphs or graphics. Simply click where you want to place the text and begin typing. You can create special pages such as title pages more quickly this way.

Configuring the shadow cursor

To select options for the shadow cursor, follow these steps:

1. Choose Tools⇨Settings or press Alt+F12 to open the "Settings" dialog box.
2. Click Display to open the "Display Settings" dialog box.
3. Select the Document tab.
4. Choose options in the shadow cursor area of the Document tab.
5. Click OK or press Enter to close the "Display Settings" dialog box; then click Close to exit the "Settings" dialog box and return to the current document.

Turning the shadow cursor off and on

Choose View⇨Shadow Cursor.

Spell-As-You-Go

(See "Proofread" earlier in this part.)

Status Bar

(See "Application Bar" earlier in this part.)

Toolbars

The toolbars let you select WordPerfect 9 commands, launch new programs, or play macros by simply displaying the correct toolbar and then clicking the correct button.

Show me the toolbars!

You can choose which toolbars appear in the program window by following these steps:

1. Choose View⇨Toolbars to open the "Toolbars" dialog box.

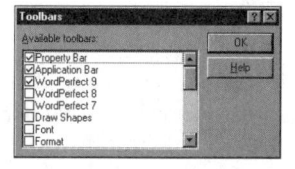

[Screenshot of Toolbars dialog box showing Available toolbars list: Property Bar, Application Bar, WordPerfect 9 (checked), WordPerfect 8, WordPerfect 7, Draw Shapes, Font, Format; with OK and Help buttons.]

2. Select the toolbar by placing a check mark next to its name.

3. Click OK to close the "Toolbars" dialog box.

TIP: You can move the toolbar by positioning the mouse pointer on the toolbar (preferably in a gray space where no buttons exist). When the mouse pointer changes to a four-headed arrow, you can drag the toolbar to a new position and drop it. Toolbars can be anchored to any side of the document window and can also float in the document window when dragged there.

Button up that toolbar!

Toolbars are probably the most customizable features in WordPerfect 9. To make toolbar alterations, follow these steps:

1. Click any toolbar with the secondary mouse button.

2. On the QuickMenu that opens, choose Settings to open the "Customize Settings" dialog box.

Toolbars

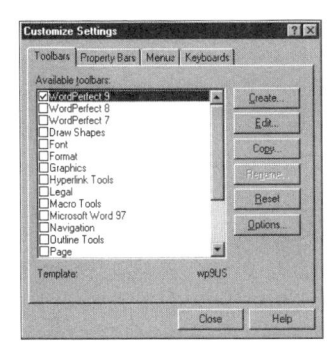

The "Customize Settings" dialog box contains these toolbar-related tabs:

- **Toolbars:** Change how the toolbar looks or specify a new one.
- **Property Bars:** Change how the Property bar looks and change its position in the document window.

3. Click Options on the Toolbars or Property Bars tab to open the "Toolbar Options" or "Property Bar Options" dialog box.

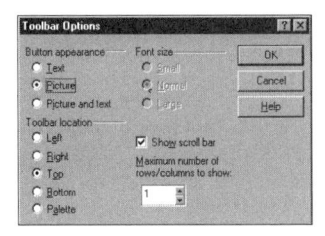

4. Choose from the following options:

- **Button appearance:** Display button as pictures, text, or both.
- **Font size:** Select the relative size of text for buttons on the Toolbar or Property bar.
- **Toolbar location:** Display the toolbar on the left, right, top, or bottom of the document window; or display it as a floating palette in the document window.
- **Show scroll bar:** Display the scroll bar if the toolbar extends beyond the screen.
- **Maximum number of rows/columns to show:** Determine how many rows of buttons display at the top of the document window.

Toolbars

5. Click OK or press Enter to close the "Options" dialog box.

6. Click Close to return to the document window.

Create a custom toolbar

WordPerfect 9 allows you to easily create your own toolbars from the available default toolbars. Follow these steps:

1. Display the toolbar you want to customize if it's not already open (see "Show me the toolbars!" earlier in this part).

2. Click the toolbar with the secondary mouse button and then choose Edit from the QuickMenu that appears.

WordPerfect 9 opens a Toolbar Editor for whichever toolbar you select to customize.

3. Choose from these tabs in the dialog box:

- **Features:** Add a feature to a toolbar button. Select a feature category and then select a feature.

- **Keystrokes:** Add a toolbar button that types the keystrokes you specify.

- **Programs:** Add a button to a toolbar that runs a selected program.

- **Macros:** Add a button to a toolbar that runs a selected macro.

4. After you finish customizing the toolbar, click OK or press Enter to close the Toolbar Editor and return to the document window.

> **TIP:** Unlike Property bars (see the "Property Bar" section earlier in this part), which can have keyboard shortcuts so that you don't have to use a mouse to select buttons, buttons on a toolbar are accessible only by clicking the primary mouse button.

Desktop Publishing

Part VI

Once upon a time, if you wanted a flyer, newsletter, or brochure, you had to go to a printer or service bureau and pay them big bucks to get your word out on the streets. Desktop computers have broken the stranglehold that these businesses had on producing professional-looking documents. For better or worse, it's up to all you fledgling desktop publishers to uphold the fine layout and printing standards that expert printers have set forth. Fortunately, WordPerfect 9 gives you the tools needed to do just that.

In this part . . .

- ✔ **Getting graphic with a document**
- ✔ **Taming text blocks by using "Keep Text Together"**
- ✔ **Inserting tables**
- ✔ **Sorting**
- ✔ **Using the Make It Fit Expert**
- ✔ **Dealing with watermarks, widows, and orphans**

Advance

(See "Typesetting" later in this part.)

Block Protect

(See "Keep Text Together" later in this part.)

Conditional End of Page

(See "Keep Text Together" later in this part.)

Graphics (Boxes)

This tool lets you dress up a document by inserting clip art, charts, graphs, scanned photographs, and decorative text. When you insert an image, it is placed inside a box (sometimes called a *frame*) that you click to select. A selected box is indicated by sizing handles (those little black squares that appear around the borders of the graphics box).

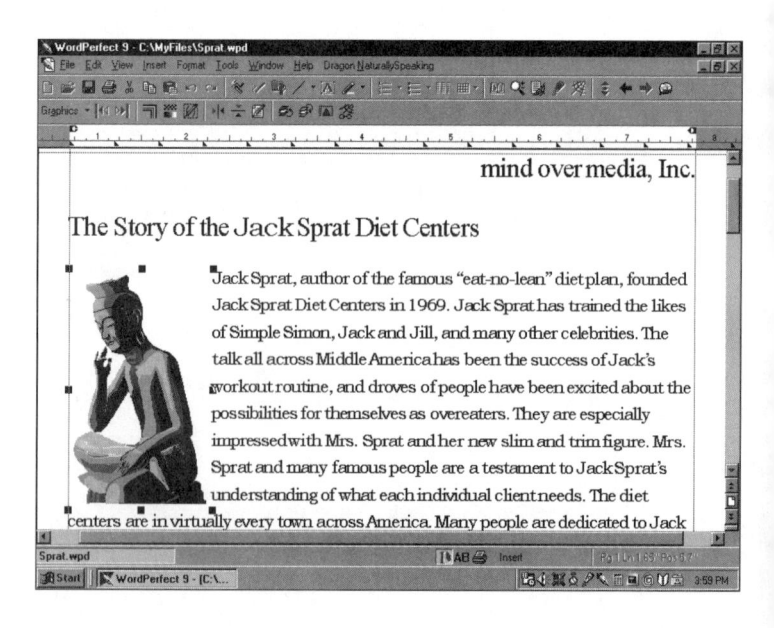

Graphics (Boxes)

Getting graphic

To insert graphic elements into a document, follow these steps:

1. Choose Insert➪Graphics.

2. Select from these options on the Graphics menu:

- **Clipart:** Place an image from the WordPerfect 9 Scrapbook.
- **From File:** Place clip art or graphics from another file.
- **TextArt:** Create special effects and decorative text.
- **Draw Picture:** Create a drawing.
- **Chart:** Create a chart.
- **Acquire Image:** Scan an image.
- **Select Image Source:** Select a scanner.
- **Custom Box:** Create a custom graphics box.

After you select one of the above options, an appropriate dialog box opens so that you can select, edit, or create an image.

3. In most cases, after you've finished selecting a graphic element, click Insert to place the graphic in the document.

When you select an image from the WordPerfect 9 Scrapbook, you only have to drag and drop the image from the Scrapbook to the open document.

You can do a lot of on-the-fly editing to graphics boxes after you insert them into a document by using the Graphics QuickMenu. To display the Graphics QuickMenu, click a graphics box with the secondary mouse button to select the box and display the menu. The Graphics QuickMenu contains lots of useful commands that let you do neat things, such as add captions, edit selected graphics, and change borders and fill patterns in the graphics box. It also lets you change the way text wraps in relation to the graphics box.

Little boxes with style

When you insert an image into your document, as outlined in the preceding section, WordPerfect 9 puts the graphics file in a figure box. In addition to a figure box, WordPerfect 9 offers a host of other box styles from which you can choose, each of which offers a slightly different option.

To choose another type of graphics box for the image you have added, follow these steps:

Graphics (Boxes)

1. Choose Insert⇨Graphics⇨Custom Box to open the "Custom Box" dialog box.

The "Custom Box" dialog box is used to create a graphics box with any available box style.

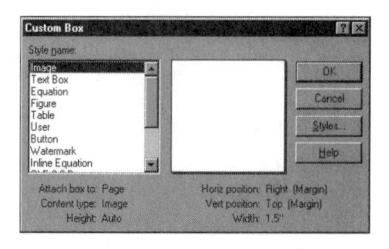

2. Click Styles to open the "Box Styles" dialog box.

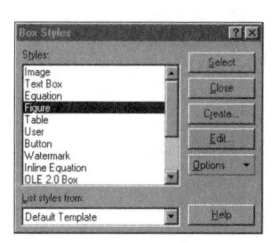

3. In the "Styles" list box, select the style type that you want to customize.

4. Choose Options⇨Copy.

5. Type a name for the new style and then click OK.

6. Select the new style, click Edit, and modify any options for the style that you just copied.

The "Edit Box Style" dialog box opens.

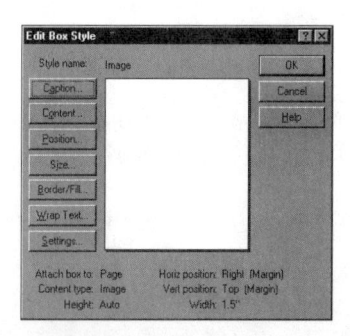

Graphics (Boxes)

7. After you finish creating the custom box style, click OK to close the "Edit Box Style" dialog box.

8. Click Select in the "Box Styles" dialog box to insert your new box style into the document, or click Close to close the "Box Styles" dialog box.

   WordPerfect 9 adds your new style to the Styles list for future use.

> **TIP:** You can use the shadow cursor to drag across a blank area of your document. This displays a QuickMenu that lets you insert any type of graphics box, including clip art, text boxes, tables, and other custom boxes.

Moving and sizing graphics boxes

After you have your graphics box in the document, you may find that you want to move the box around or make it bigger or smaller. If you're a mouse maniac, WordPerfect 9 makes this process a snap. To move the box, just select it and drag it to its new position in the document. To resize the box, click it to make the sizing handles appear. Pick a sizing handle and begin dragging it until the box is the size and shape you want. Then release the mouse button.

> **TIP:** To get rid of a graphics box, click the box to select it and press Delete to zap it out of existence.

Editing graphics

You can do no end of editing and playing around with a graphics image inside its graphics box. To do so, click the graphics box with the secondary mouse button and choose Image Tools on the QuickMenu.

142 Guidelines

The Image Tools palette is then displayed next to the graphics box. To see what each tool does, click the tool button with the secondary mouse button and read the QuickTip description that appears.

Guidelines

Guidelines show the margins or measurements of elements in a document, such as page margins, tables, columns, headers, and footers. Guidelines appear in the document window as dotted lines, but they do not print in the document.

To view guidelines, choose View➪Guidelines.

FAST TRACK You can change the structure of the document by dragging a guideline to a new position. This is the quickest way to change margins, size tables or columns, or place headers and footers on the page.

Keep Text Together

You can keep sections of text from being split apart on different pages of a document. WordPerfect 9 offers several methods for doing so:

1. Choose Format➪Keep Text Together to open the "Keep Text Together" dialog box.

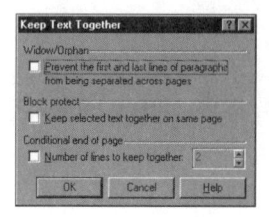

2. Choose from the following options:

- **Widow/Orphan:** Prevents the first or last line of a paragraph from being split apart across pages.

- **Block protect:** Keeps the block of selected text from ever being split apart on different pages.

- **Conditional end of page:** Keeps a specified number of lines together on a page; you enter in the text box the number of lines you want to keep together (as counted down from the insertion point's current position).

> **TIP:** If you want to keep a title with its first paragraph or a table of data together and you don't know the number of lines to specify, select all the text and then place a check next to "Keep selected text together on same page" under "Block protect."

Line Height

This feature lets you control how much blank space WordPerfect 9 puts between each line of text on a page (something the program normally takes care of automatically).

To change line height in a document, follow these steps:

1. Choose Format⇨Line⇨Height to open the "Line Height" dialog box.

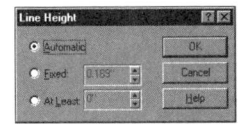

2. Select from these radio buttons to set line height:

- **Automatic:** Use the default line height for the current font. Line height is the distance between the top of one line of text and the top of the next line of text.

- **Fixed:** Use a fixed (rather than flexible) line height. Enter the new measurement (as measured from the baseline of one line to the baseline of the next line) in the text box or use the scroll list buttons.

- **At Least:** Set a minimum line height measurement to keep line spacing even when you have different sizes of text in your document.

3. Click OK or press Enter.

Most of the time, you don't have to monkey around with the line height. WordPerfect 9 automatically increases the height as necessary to accommodate the largest font you use in a line. Once in a blue moon, however, you may have a situation in which you want to increase or decrease the amount of space between certain lines of text without changing the line spacing.

> **TIP:** When you fix the line height, the new height remains in effect for all subsequent lines in the document. If you reach a place where you want WordPerfect 9 to determine the best line height for your text,

place the insertion point at the beginning of the line. Then open the "Line Height" dialog box and this time choose the "Automatic" radio button.

Make It Fit

This command lets you puff up or shrink the text and graphics in your document so that they fit within a set number of pages.

The Make It Fit feature is great for things like cramming a two-page resume onto one page. Follow these steps:

1. Choose Format➪Make It Fit to open the "Make It Fit" dialog box.

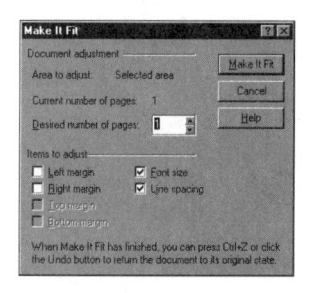

2. Choose from the following features:

   - **Desired number of pages:** Specify how many filled pages WordPerfect needs to expand or compress the document text to fit into.
   - **Left margin:** Increase or decrease the left margin as required to make the document fit in the specified number of pages.
   - **Right margin:** Increase or decrease the right margin as required to make the document fit in the specified number of pages.
   - **Top margin:** Increase or decrease the top margin as required to make the document fit in the specified number of pages.
   - **Bottom margin:** Increase or decrease the bottom margin as required to make the document fit in the specified number of pages.
   - **Font size:** Increase or decrease the size of the fonts used in the text as required to make the document fit in the specified number of pages.

- **Line spacing:** Increase or decrease the line spacing used in the text as required to make the document fit in the specified number of pages.

(WordPerfect 9 New!) In WordPerfect 9, the Make It Fit feature is enhanced to allow compression or expansion of not only full pages, but also selected sections of your document. Just select the text block that you want to expand or compress and apply the Make It Fit feature as described in the preceding section. WordPerfect fits the text block into a given dimension without affecting other areas where fitting specifications may be different.

(TIP) To restore your document to its original page count, should your Make It Fit endeavor end in disaster, use Undo (Ctrl+Z). You might also do yourself a favor and choose File➪Save As to save the resized document as a separate file under a new name (so that you always have access to the original) before you try printing your expanded or compressed version.

Paragraph Format

This option lets you indent the first line of a paragraph, change the spacing between paragraphs, and adjust the left and right margins of a paragraph (without adjusting the margins of the document).

Paragraph formatting can be really useful in a desktop publishing project. Follow these steps:

1. Place the insertion point in the first paragraph you want to format.

2. Choose Format➪Paragraph➪Format to open the "Paragraph Format" dialog box.

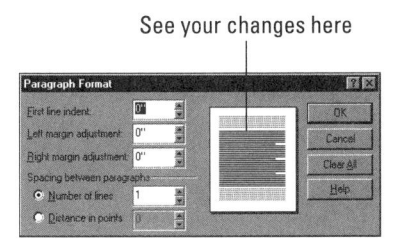

See your changes here

3. Choose from the following options:

- **First line indent:** Specify how far to indent only the first line of each paragraph.

- **Left margin adjustment:** Indent the left edge of each paragraph without changing the left margin for the document.
- **Right margin adjustment:** Indent the right edge of each paragraph without changing the right margin for the document.
- **Spacing between paragraphs:** Adjust the spacing between paragraphs (one line by default).
  - **Number of lines:** Specify a number to represent a multiple of the current line spacing. For example, if line spacing is set at 1.5, specifying 2 for paragraph spacing inserts 3 lines after each paragraph.
  - **Distance in points:** Specify the number of points you want between paragraphs. 72 points are in one inch.
- **Clear All:** Return to the default paragraph format settings.

4. Click OK or press Enter to close the "Paragraph Format" dialog box.

> **TIP:** If you reach a point in the document where you want to return to normal formatting, place the insertion point in that paragraph. Then open the "Paragraph Format" dialog box and click Clear All.

Reference

The Reference menu commands let you mark text to create lists for various long form documents.

Choose Tools⇨Reference to view these commands on the Reference menu:

✦ **List:** Define and mark items for a list.

✦ **Index:** Define and mark items for an index.

✦ **Cross-Reference:** Mark cross-references.

✦ **Table of Contents:** Define and mark items and generate a table of contents.

✦ **Table of Authorities:** Define and mark items and generate a table of authorities for a legal brief.

Reference 147

Creating lists in WordPerfect 9 requires three basic procedures:

- ✦ Mark the text to include in the list.
- ✦ Define the way you want the list to look (called a *list definition*).
- ✦ Generate the list.

When you choose a list command on the Reference menu, the corresponding toolbar appears to help you through the list-building process.

The following steps show you how to easily create a full range of lists:

1. Choose Tools⇨Reference⇨List.

2. Type the name of the list in the List text box on the List toolbar.

List toolbar

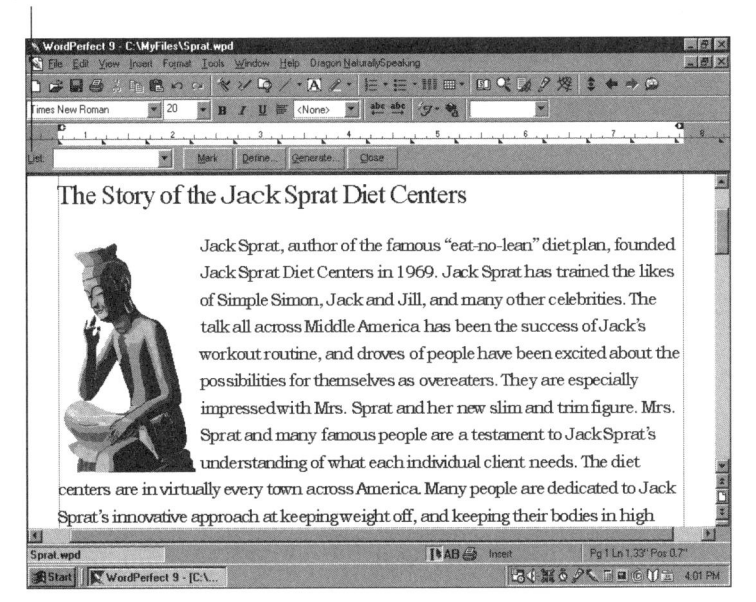

3. Select a word or phrase in the document that you want to include as an entry in the list.

4. Click Mark.

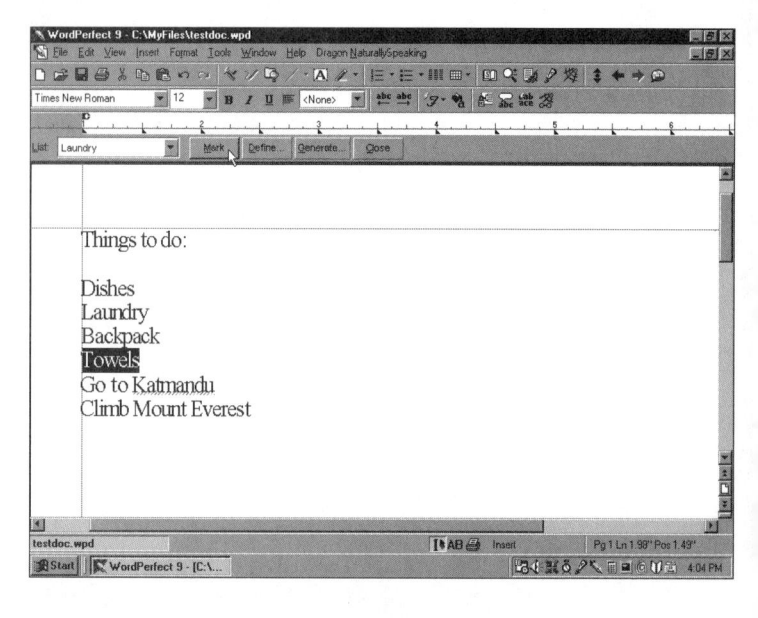

5. Repeat Steps 3 and 4 for each item you want to include in the list.

6. Click where you want the list to appear in your document.

7. Click Define to open the "Define List" dialog box.

The "Define List" dialog box contains the names of previously defined lists, plus the options needed for creating, editing, retrieving, or deleting list definitions.

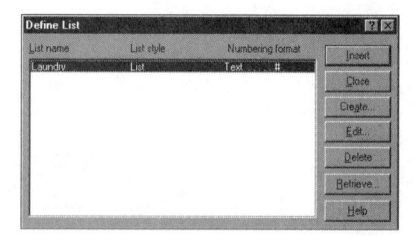

8. Click a List name and then click Insert.

9. On the List toolbar, click Generate to open the "Generate" dialog box.

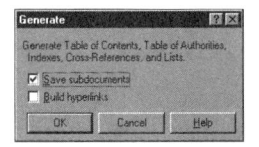

Shapes 149

10. Choose from the following options on the "Generate" dialog box:

- **Save subdocuments:** Lets you save changes to subdocuments when the document is generated.
- **Build hyperlinks:** Creates and generates hyperlinks from any item on your list to any marked text.

11. Click OK or press Enter to generate your list and then click Close on the List toolbar to hide the toolbar.

> **TIP:** To start the list at the top of a new page, press Ctrl+Enter.

Shapes

WordPerfect 9 provides more than 100 new shapes with which to enhance your documents. You can choose shapes from any of the new shape palettes in the "Draw Object Shapes" dialog box. To become an expert shape shifter, follow these steps:

1. Choose Insert⇔Shapes to open the "Draw Object Shapes" dialog box.

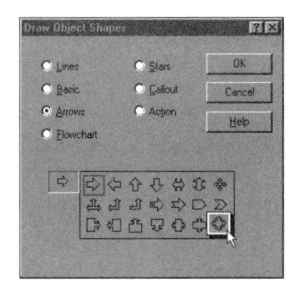

2. Click a radio button to display the following palettes in the "Draw Object Shapes" dialog box:

- **Lines:** Change the cursor to a line drawing tool. Be your own Piet Mondrian.
- **Basic:** Twenty-four basic shapes and symbols.
- **Arrows:** A palette of multi-directional arrows.

- **Flowchart:** More flowcharting components than you'll probably ever need.
- **Stars:** A palette full of complex polygons (none from Hollywood) and banners.
- **Callout:** Callout shapes have pointers that can be anchored anywhere in the document.
- **Action:** Action buttons prompt the assignment of an action lik playing a sound, movie, or macro.

3. Float the cursor over a shape palette to preview a shape, and then click to select it.

4. Click OK or press Enter to close the "Draw Object Shapes" dialog box and return to the current document.

The cursor changes to a drawing tool in the current document.

5. Drag, and release the mouse button at a desired location in the document to insert the shape.

After you insert a shape, you can drag it, size it, and wrap text around it. You can also edit the shapes until you're blue in the face. Even add drop shadows. To perform any of these (and more) editing functions, just click the shape with the secondary mouse button and access all the great editing tools on the QuickMenu.

All shapes have the new Text In Shapes feature, which allows text to be added into the shape on-the- fly. Click a shape with the secondary mouse and choose Add Text on the QuickMenu. Begin typing in the text box that appears on the shape.

Sort

This command lets you rearrange text in alphabetic or numeric order.

It takes all sorts

Sorting is based on keys that indicate what specific information should be used to alphabetize or numerically reorder the text. You may have a list that contains your coworkers' names and telephone numbers, for example, and you want to sort the list alphabetically by last name. You tell WordPerfect 9 to use the last name of each person as the sorting key. When you sort information with WordPerfect 9, you can define more than one sorting key. If your list of names and telephone numbers contains several Smiths and Joneses, you can define a second key that indicates how you want the duplicates to be arranged (by first name, for example).

To sort information in WordPerfect 9, follow these steps:

1. Select the lines or paragraphs that you want to sort.

2. Choose Tools⇨Sort or press Alt+F9 to open the "Sort" dialog box.

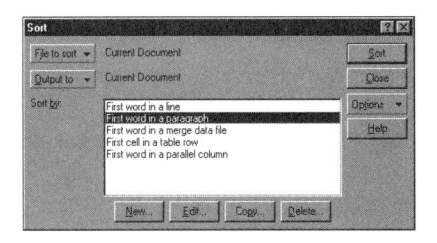

3. Choose from the following options:

- **File to sort:** Specify the location of the data to be sorted.
- **Output to:** Specify the location where you want to display the sorted data.
- **Sort by:** Select a default or user-defined sorting rule.
- **New:** Define a new sorting system in the "New Sort" dialog box.
- **Edit:** Change an existing sort definition.
- **Copy:** Change an existing definition but also keep the original definition.
- **Delete:** Delete the selected sort definition.
- **Options:** Select Allow Undo after sorting to return sorted text to its original order after you have sorted it. Select Uppercase sorts before lowercase to sort uppercase letters before lowercase letters.

4. Click Sort to perform the selected sort and return to the open document.

Sorting out the sorts

The key to understanding sorting in WordPerfect 9 is to understand that the program divides information into fields and records, based on the different types of sorts found in the "Sort" dialog box:

✦ **First word in a line:** Each line terminated by a hard return is considered to be a record.

✦ **First word in a paragraph:** Each paragraph that ends in two or more hard returns is a record.

- ✦ **First word in a merge data file:** Each record ends with an ENDRECORD merge code.
- ✦ **First cell in a table row:** Each record is one row.
- ✦ **First word in a parallel column:** Each record is one row of parallel columns. (See "Columns" in Part III.)

Tables

This tool lets you set text in a tabular format by using a layout of columns and rows.

Creating a table

To create a table, first indicate the number of columns and rows that the table should have by following these steps:

1. Move the insertion point to the beginning of the new line in the document where you want the table to appear.

2. Choose Insert⇨Table or press F12 to open the "Create Table" dialog box.

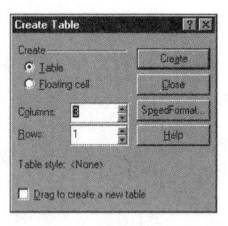

3. Choose from these options:

- **Table:** Create a table structured with rows and columns.
- **Floating cell:** Create a floating cell that can be linked to other parts of the document.
- **Columns:** Specify the number of vertical columns for the table
- **Rows:** Specify the number of horizontal rows for the table.
- **Drag to create a new table:** Drag to create a table of any size wherever you click the shadow cursor. Click to clear this option in order to create tables at the insertion point that span the page width.
- **SpeedFormat:** Select a predefined table style from the "Table Speed Format" dialog box.

4. Click Create or press Enter.

Click the Table QuickCreate button on the WordPerfect 9 toolbar (see "Toolbars" in Part V for details) and drag through the tiny table grid until you have highlighted all the cells you want in the table. Then release the mouse button.

To change the width or height of a column in a table, position the mouse pointer somewhere on the border of the column you want to change. When the pointer changes to a double-headed arrow, drag the column border until the column is the size you want.

Entering text in a table

After creating the table structure, you can enter text in the various cells of the table. To enter text, position the insertion point in the cell (it's in the first cell by default) and begin typing. To advance to the next cell on the right, press Tab. To return to the preceding cell, press Shift+Tab (which is a backward tab). When you reach the last cell in a row, pressing Tab moves you to the cell at the beginning of the next row. If you press Tab when the insertion point is in the last cell of a table, WordPerfect 9 adds a blank row of cells to the table and positions the insertion point in the first cell in this new row.

The Table QuickMenu, which you can see when you click your secondary mouse button, enables you to do lots of table-related stuff, such as format existing cells or insert or delete cells. You can also use the QuickMenu to display tools for creating a rudimentary spreadsheet complete with row and column headings, as well as a formula bar to use when you create and calculate formulas in the cells.

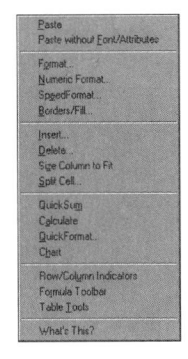

Skewed table cells

This new feature in WordPerfect 9 lets you skew (slant) the top row or the left or right column of a table. To skew cells in a table, do the following:

1. Right-click in the table and choose F_ormat on the QuickMenu to open the "Properties for Table Format" dialog box.

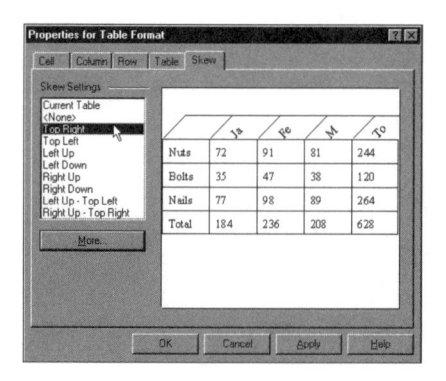

2. Click the Skew tab and select from these options:

   - **Skew Settings:** Use this area to choose the part of the table that you want skewed.

   - **More:** Click this button to access the "Edit Skew" dialog box, where you can change the angle of the skew and square the edge of the first or last column to prevent the cells from extending beyond the edge of the table. Text that you type in a skewed cell is automatically slanted. To prevent text from slanting, click to remove the check mark in the "S_kew Text" check box.

3. Click OK or press Enter to close the "Edit Skew" dialog box.

4. Click _Apply to see skew results in the preview area of the "Properties for Table Format" dialog box.

5. Click OK or press Enter to close the "Properties for Table Format" dialog box and return to the current document.

Turn off skewing

To remove the skew in a table:

1. Right-click the table and select F_ormat on the QuickMenu to open the "Properties for Table Format" dialog box.

2. Choose <None> from the Skew Settings list.

3. Click OK or press Enter to close the "Properties for Table Format" dialog box and return to the current document.

TIP: You may need to increase the row height of a skewed row to accommodate the text. For information about changing the height of a row, see the Tip in "Creating a table," earlier in this part.

Typesetting

The Typesetting menu gives you great tools for creating desktop publishing projects. Choose Format⇨Typesetting to see this menu.

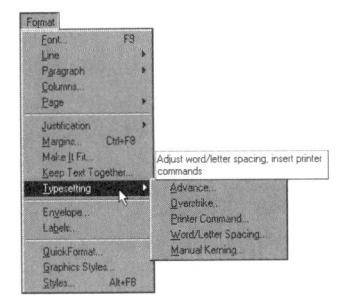

The following list gives you the lowdown on these menu commands:

- **Advance:** Positions text precisely on the page without requiring you to monkey around with tabs, spaces, and hard returns.
- **Overstrike:** Creates an overstrike character (one that combines two or more characters into one) in the "Overstrike" dialog box.
- **Printer Command:** Inserts commands that let you take advantage of the special functions of your printer.
- **Word/Letter Spacing:** Adjusts word/letter spacing, line heights, and other options in the "Word/Letter Spacing" dialog box.
- **Manual Kerning:** Increases or decreases the space between two characters in the "Manual Kerning" dialog box.

Watermarks

This tool inserts background text or graphics in a document that can still be read after other text is printed over it.

Creating a watermark is similar to creating a header or footer. To create a watermark, follow these steps:

1. Place the insertion point on the first page where you want to have a watermark.

2. Choose Insert⇨Watermark to open the "Watermark" dialog box.

3. Click Create to create Watermark A. (To create a second watermark, select Watermark B before you click Create.)

WordPerfect 9 opens a special Watermark window where you create the watermark.

4. To add a graphics image to the watermark, drag in the document to create a graphics box (see "Graphics (Boxes)" earlier in this part).

5. To add text to your watermark, type the text in the Watermark window or open the document that contains the text.

6. After you finish entering and formatting the watermark text or adding the watermark graphics images, click the Close button on the Watermark Property Bar.

The Watermark window and Watermark Property Bar both close, and you return to your document.

> **TIP:** Any watermark you add to a document is visible on the screen only when the program is in Page view or Two Page view. When you switch to Draft view, the watermark image and text disappear from the screen.

You can suppress the printing of a watermark on a specific page just as you can suppress a header or footer from printing (see the "Header/Footer" section in Part II for details).

Widow/Orphan

(See "Keep Text Together" earlier in this part.)

Web Publishing

Part VII

Web publishing. The very sound of the term makes you feel like you, too, can be a part of the great migration to the World Wide Web that embodies the height (hype?) of coolness in the dawn light of a new millennium. Of course, you may just want to collaborate with your other-coast buddies on the company intranet or create a family Web page for Aunt Sylvia in Enid, Oklahoma. Whatever the case, this part shows you how WordPerfect 9 can transform you into a Web-meister with any degree of competency you aspire to.

In this part . . .

- Getting hyper about hyperlinks
- Using SpeedLinks
- Creating a Web document of your own
- Creating a fancy Web document of your own
- Converting WordPerfect 9 documents to HTML
- Seeing your Web document in a real browser

Hyperlink

Hyperlinks allow you to jump automatically to another part of a WordPerfect document, to a Web page on the Internet, or to your company's intranet.

Creating a hyperlink

To create a hyperlink, follow these steps:

1. Select the words or symbols that you want to use as the link.
2. Choose Tools⇨Hyperlink to open the "Hyperlink Properties" dialog box.

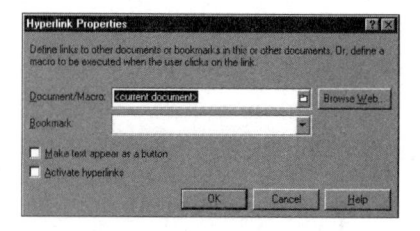

3. Choose from the following options:

   - **Document/Macro:** Select the current document or another file as the hyperlink.
   - **Bookmark:** Select a bookmark in another document as the hyperlink.
   - **Make text appear as a button:** Causes hyperlinks to appear as buttons.
   - **Activate hyperlinks:** Turn on all hyperlinks in the current document.
   - **Browse Web:** Launch your browser and then go to the desired document. The URL (Uniform Resource Locator) address of that document is inserted into the Document/Macro text box when you close the browser.

4. After you finish defining the hyperlink, click OK or press Enter to insert the hyperlink into the current document.

Hyperlink

When you return to the current document, the new hyperlink appears in blue text. If you float the mouse pointer over the hyperlink, a QuickTip displays the path to the linked document. Just click the hyperlink to be transported to your chosen destination.

- ✦ If you want to create a hyperlink to a local Web document, specify the path and filename that you want to link to in the Document/Macro text box.

- ✦ If you want to create a link to a bookmark in a non-HTML document, click a name on the Bookmark drop-down list. See "Internet Publisher" later in this part for more about HTML.

TIP: If you type a URL address in the Document/Macro text box and then click Browse Web, the browser attempts to locate the document for you.

Editing a hyperlink

To edit a hyperlink, you must deactivate it. To do so, follow these steps:

1. Choose Tools⇔Hyperlink.

   The "Hyperlink Properties" dialog box opens.

2. Click to remove the check mark in the "Activate hyperlink" check box.

3. Click OK to close the "Hyperlink Properties" dialog box.

4. Make any editing changes to the hyperlink.

5. After you're finished editing the hyperlink, reopen the "Hyperlink Properties" dialog box and click to place a check mark in the "Activate hyperlink" check box.

Using SpeedLinks

Use SpeedLinks to create links to Web documents that you go to all the time. Here's how:

1. Choose Tools⇔QuickCorrect to open the "QuickCorrect" dialog box.

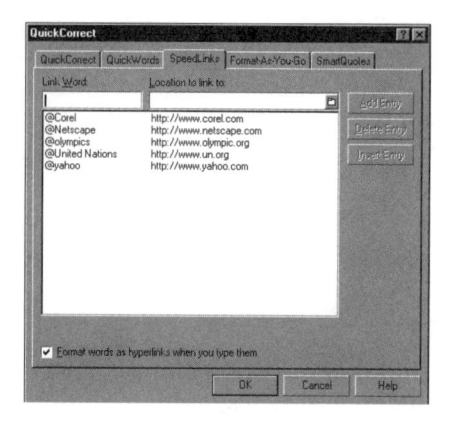

2. Select the SpeedLinks tab.

3. Type the word that you want converted to a SpeedLink in the Link Word text box.

   If you preselected a word for the hyperlink in the document, it appears in the Link Word text box.

4. Type the associated URL in the Location to link to text box.

5. Click Insert Entry.

Use the "Format words as hyperlinks when you type them" check box to turn SpeedLinks off and on.

TIP Use SpeedLinks to set up frequently used links. For example, I specify that typing **@Mind** automatically sets up a link to my home page. www.mindovermedia.com.

CROSS-REFERENCE For more information about this command, see Chapter 18 of *WordPerfect 9 For Windows For Dummies*.

Internet Publisher

Most documents published on the Internet are written in HyperText Markup Language, or HTML. The WordPerfect 9 Internet Publisher converts a WordPerfect document to HTML, allowing anyone with an HTML browser such as Netscape Navigator or Microsoft Internet Explorer to read your document.

Internet Publisher supports most HTML 2.0, 3.0, and 3.2 tags and allows you to use certain browser-specific HTML tags defined for Netscape Navigator or Microsoft Internet Explorer.

Internet Publisher 161

Creating a new Web page

To create a new Web page with the Internet Publisher:

1. Choose File⇨Internet Publisher to open the "Internet Publisher" dialog box.

2. Click the New Web Document button in the "Internet Publisher" dialog box.

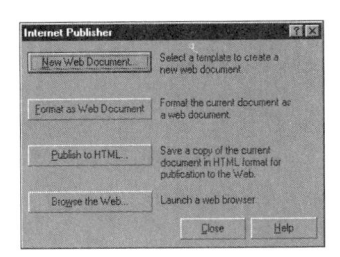

3. Click the Select button to choose the default new Web document in the "Select New Web Document" dialog box to open a blank Web document in the document window.

4. Click the PerfectExpert button on the WordPerfect 9 toolbar to open the Internet Publisher PerfectExpert. The figure below shows (for better viewing in this tiny book) how the Corel PerfectExpert appears when it is undocked from its default location on the left side of the document window.

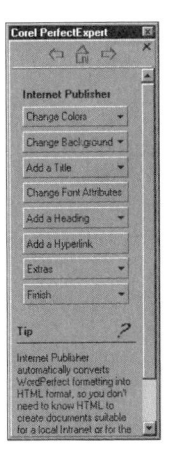

The Internet Publisher PerfectExpert is your personal guide to creating stunning Web documents for publishing on the Internet.

5. Choose from the following options:

- **Change Colors**: Choose text, links, and background colors.
- **Change Background:** Choose from a variety of default background patterns or create a custom background pattern, because gray is *sooo* boring.
- **Add a Title:** Open the Title tab of the "HTML Document Properties" dialog box so that you can use the first heading in the document for a title or create a custom title.
- **Change Font Attributes:** "Open the Font" dialog box so you can change the font attributes in the Web document.
- **Add a Heading:** Select a heading from the standard HTML heading formats.
- **Add a Hyperlink:** Open the "Hyperlink Properties" dialog box to add a hyperlink to the Web document.
- **Extras:** Add tables, lists, and graphic lines to the Web document.
- **Finish:** View the document in your browser or save a copy in HTML.

6. After you finish setting up the Web document, click Finish to view your work in a browser or save it as an HTML file for publishing on the Internet.

To format the current document as a Web document, click the Change View button on the WordPerfect 9 toolbar.

The following are some down and dirty techniques for adding zip to your Web document by using the Internet Publisher PerfectExpert.

Adding graphics to a Web page

1. Choose Extras⇨Add a Graphic from Scrapbook or Add a Graphic from file.
2. Select a graphic from the Scrapbook or file containing graphics. (You can also access graphics from a CD-ROM.)
3. Click Insert.

   If you are inserting graphics from the Scrapbook, you can simply drag and drop them.

Internet Publisher 163

Creating a table on the Web page

1. Choose Extras⇨Add a Table.
2. Format the table in the "HTML Table Format" dialog box.

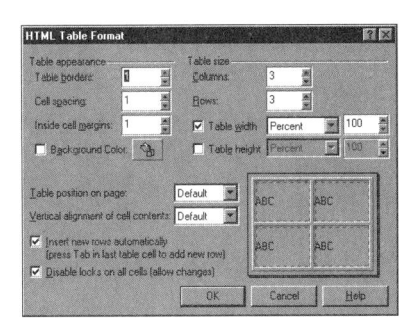

3. Click OK to insert the table into the Web document.

The table appears in the Web document window. If you select a cell in the table, the Table Property Bar appears:

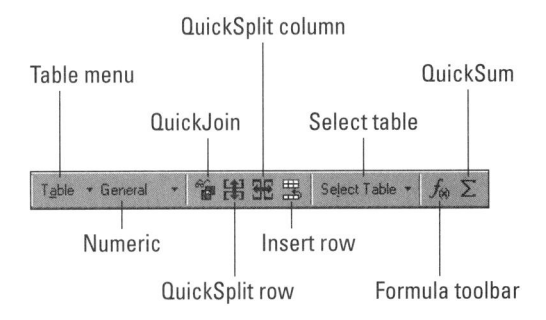

- Table menu
- QuickJoin
- QuickSplit column
- Select table
- QuickSum
- Numeric
- QuickSplit row
- Insert row
- Formula toolbar

You can continue to format the table by using the Table Property Bar, view and edit formulas, and perform QuickSum operations.

Adding lists to the Web page

1. Choose Extras⇨Add a List.
2. Choose from the three styles in the "Bullets and Numbering" dialog box.

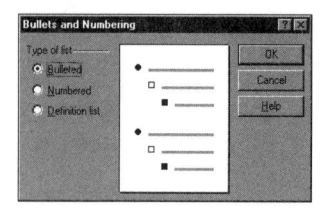

Internet Publisher

The options available in the "Bullets and Numbering" dialog box are as follows:

- Bulleted
- Numbered
- Definition list

3. Click OK or press Enter to start the list in the Web document.

Inserting horizontal rules in the Web page

1. Choose Extras⇨Add a Horizontal Line.

2. Marvel at the beauty of your horizontal line when it appears in the Web document.

Adding a form to the Web page

1. Choose Extras⇨Add a Form.

A form tag icon appears in the Web document, as well as the Forms Property Bar. Form fields such as radio buttons and check boxes are inserted between these form tags.

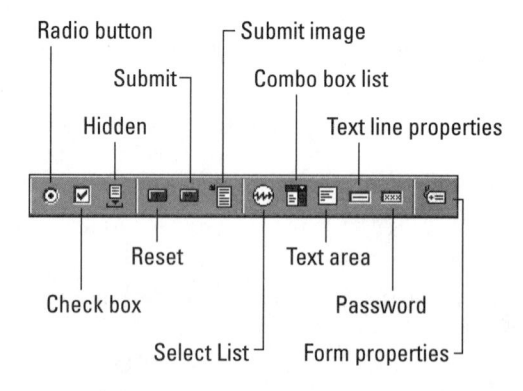

Forms Property Bar labels:
- Radio button
- Submit image
- Submit
- Combo box list
- Hidden
- Text line properties
- Reset
- Text area
- Check box
- Password
- Select List
- Form properties

2. Use the options on the Forms Property Bar to create the desired input form in the Web document.

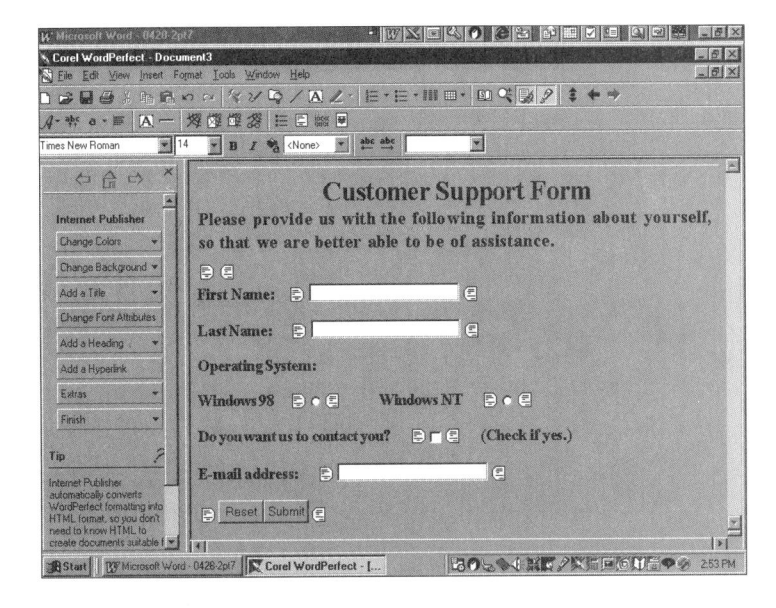

Viewing the Web document in a browser

Choose Finish⇨View in Browser.

The Internet Publisher PerfectExpert opens your registered browser and displays the Web document as it would appear when published on the Internet.

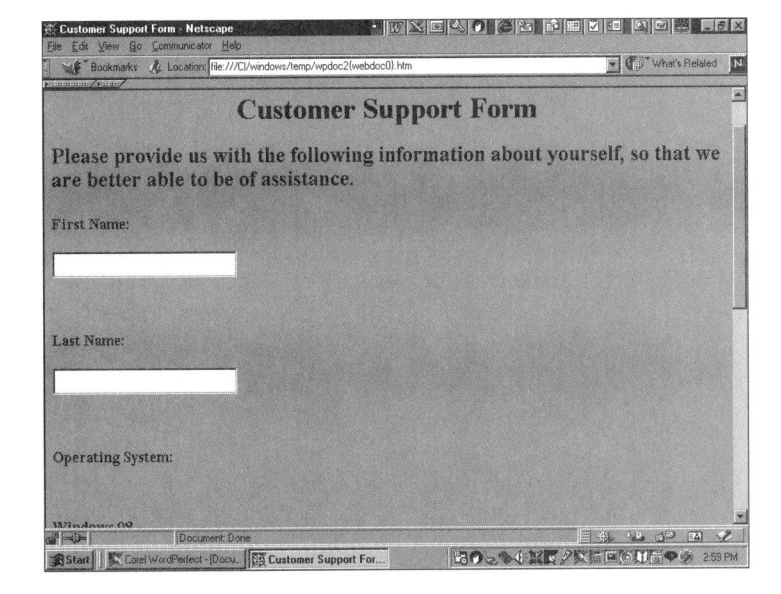

Internet Publisher

Converting a WordPerfect document into a Web page

One of the most useful Web document tools in WordPerfect 9 is the Web Editor. To use this feature, follow these steps:

1. Open the document that you want to convert into a Web document.

2. Choose File⇒Internet Publisher.

3. Click Format as a Web Document to open the Web Editor.

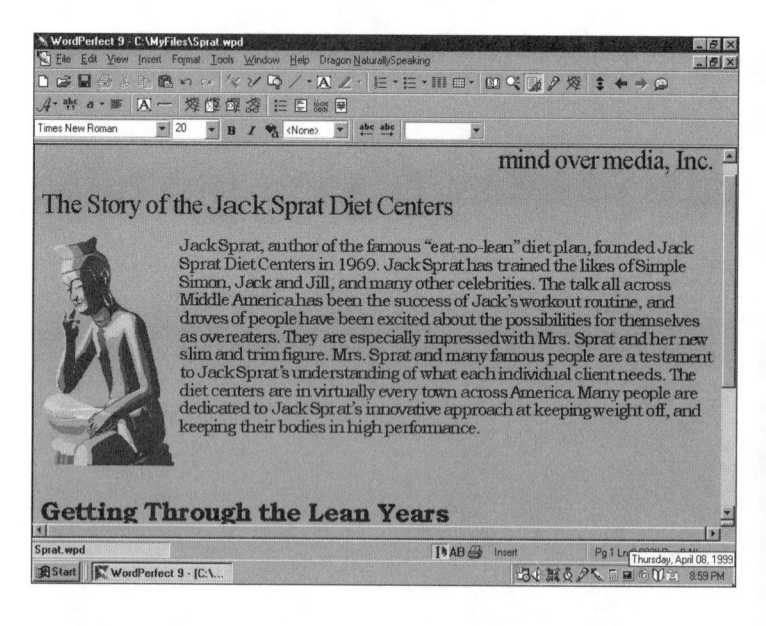

If necessary, click OK to bypass the Web View alert box.

The Web Editor formats your document as a Web document (the document background color turns browser gray) and displays the Internet Publisher toolbar.

Internet Publisher

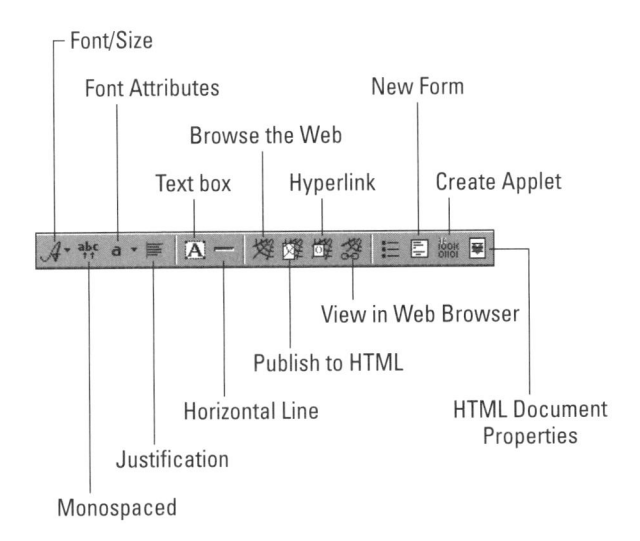

Toolbar labels:
- Font/Size
- Font Attributes
- Browse the Web
- New Form
- Text box
- Hyperlink
- Create Applet
- View in Web Browser
- Publish to HTML
- Horizontal Line
- HTML Document Properties
- Justification
- Monospaced

The Internet Publisher toolbar lets you quickly

- ✦ Open your Web browser and start surfing.
- ✦ View the current Web document in your browser of choice.
- ✦ Publish the current Web document to HTML.
- ✦ Create and edit hyperlinks.

TIP: At any time while you're editing the Web document, you can revert to a WordPerfect 9 document by choosing File➪Internet Publisher and then clicking Format as WP Document in the "Internet Publisher" dialog box. More quickly, you can click the Change View button on the WordPerfect 9 toolbar.

Saving the converted Web page

After you finish formatting the converted WordPerfect document, you can save the document as a Web page in the HTML file format, along with any graphic and sound files used on the page. Here's how:

1. In the Web Editor, choose File➪Internet Publisher or click the Publish to HTML button on the Internet Publisher toolbar to open the "Publish to HTML" dialog box.

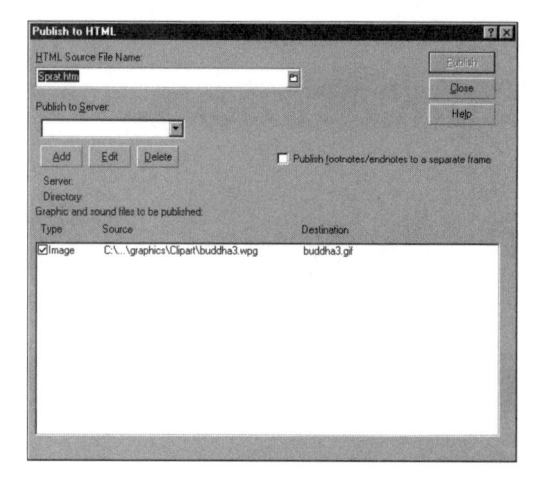

2. Use these options to define the HTML document:

- **HTML Source File Name:** Select the folder and filename for the new Web document. The default filename uses the .htm extension.

- **Publish to Server:** Select a server to store or host the new Web document. You can add or delete servers as well as edit pathnames.

- **Graphic and sound files to be published:** Lists any graphic or sound files originally embedded in the text document. Select the graphic and sound files that you want converted to Web formats (.gif for graphics and .wav for sounds) for inclusion in the new HTML document.

3. Click Publish to save the HTML document.

SpeedLinks

(See "Hyperlink" earlier in this part.)

Web Page View

Just as you can switch from Page view to Draft view and so on, WordPerfect 9 lets you see how your document will appear when it is published to HTML. To switch to Web view:

1. Choose View➪Web Page.

A Web View alert box appears, telling you that in the process of converting to Web Page view, some formatting in the document (that may not have HTML equivalents) will be lost.

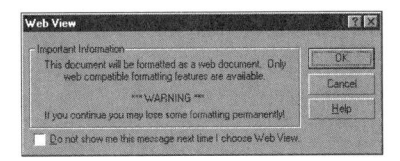

2. Click OK to acknowledge this warning.

3. View the document as it will appear when converted to a Web document.

When you format a WordPerfect 9 document for the Web, formatting codes that have no HTML equivalents are deleted or changed to HTML equivalents. If you save the document with the same filename as the original .WPD document, you lose the original formatting. Save the Web document to a new filename to preserve your original document and formatting.

Part VIII

Potpourri

You might expect by the title that Part VIII will smell wonderful because of all the dried flowers and spices I've put in. In actuality, it's just all the stuff I couldn't quite categorize into the other parts. And while the aromatic qualities of the topics may be suspect, their usefulness is not. WordPerfect 9 provides a lot of nicely unexpected features that transcend the ordinary.

In this part . . .

- ✔ **Your electronic little black address book**
- ✔ **Create a POSTNET bar code (in case you've ever wanted to)**
- ✔ **Make comments**
- ✔ **Revealing secret codes**
- ✔ **The text highlighter of your dreams**
- ✔ **Inserting sounds, spreadsheets, and databases in a document**
- ✔ **Master documents for the long-form aficionado**

Address Book

The CorelCENTRAL Address Book stores names, addresses, and phone numbers in one handy location. You can even create several different address books for various uses (home, business, and so on). You can then have the Address Book insert information into the documents you create.

Creating an address book

1. Choose Tools⇨Address Book to open the "CorelCENTRAL Address Book" dialog box.

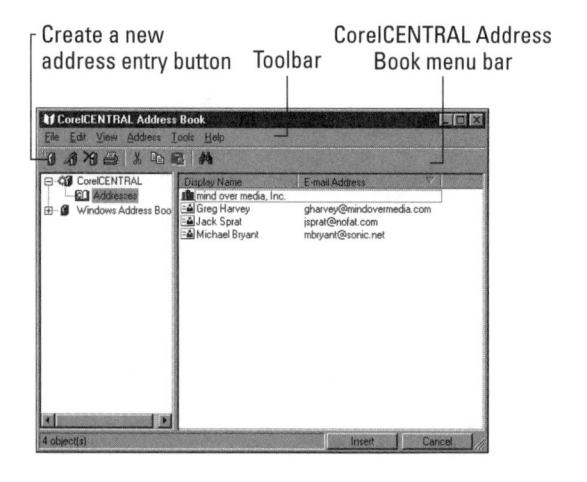

Create a new address entry button — Toolbar — CorelCENTRAL Address Book menu bar

2. Choose Address⇨New on the CorelCENTRAL Address Book menu bar or click the Create a new address entry button on the Address Book toolbar to open the "New Entry" dialog box.

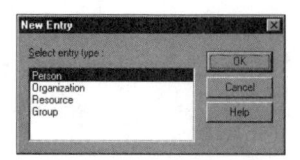

3. Select entry type (Person, for example) and click OK or press Enter to open the "New Person Properties" dialog box.

Address Book 173

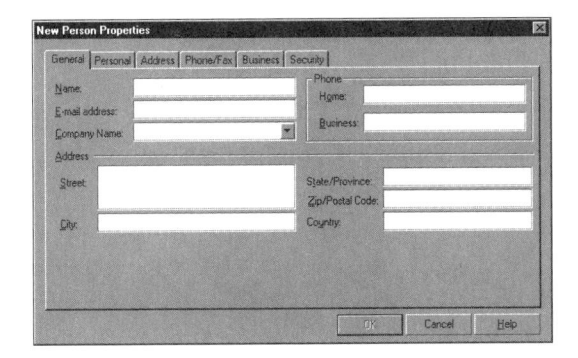

![New Person Properties dialog box with General, Personal, Address, Phone/Fax, Business, and Security tabs, showing fields for Name, E-mail address, Company Name, Street, City, Phone Home, Business, State/Province, Zip/Postal Code, and Country]

In the "New Person Properties" dialog box, you can enter a quantity of information about a person that would rival an IRS file.

4. Click OK to add the entry into the CorelCENTRAL Address Book.

Messing with your address book

After you have some entries in an address book, you can perform all sorts of useful tricks with these features on the toolbar of the "CorelCENTRAL Address Book" dialog box:

- ✦ **Create a new address book:** Create new Corel address books, Messaging Application Programming Interface (MAPI) compliant address books that allow you to work with address books you create in other programs, and directory server address books that let you access online directories.

- ✦ **Edit an address entry:** Open the "Properties" dialog box for the selected entry so you can change things.

- ✦ **Delete an address entry:** Remove an entry from the CorelCENTRAL Address Book.

These options appear on the CorelCentral Address Book menu bar:

- ✦ **Send mail:** Choose this command on the Tools menu to access Messaging Application Programming Interface (MAPI) compliant address books and e-mail programs, such as Novell GroupWise or Microsoft Outlook, to easily send e-mail.

- ✦ **Publish to HTML:** Choose this command on the File menu to create an HTML document from CorelCENTRAL Address Book entries.

- ✦ **Columns:** Choose this command on the View menu to hide or display columns of address entry information in the list of address entries.

Bar Code

+ **Filter:** Choose this command on the View menu to filter address books to show only the address entries with specific information.

+ **Insert:** Click this button to insert the selected address book entry into a document.

Bar Code

This feature lets you add a POSTNET (Postal Numeric Encoding Technique) bar code when you're addressing an envelope or creating a mailing label. A bar code is that funny-looking computer script that resembles the one food stores use to mark grocery items — which the scanners can never read. Using bar codes in your mailing addresses can save you some bucks with the post office, however, so they're worth using.

To insert a bar code in an address (or elsewhere in a document if you're really inclined), follow these steps:

1. Position the insertion point where you want the bar code to appear.

2. Choose Insert⇨Other⇨Bar code to open the "POSTNET Bar Code" dialog box.

3. Type the 11-digit delivery point bar code, 9-digit ZIP + 4, or 5-digit ZIP code in the "POSTNET Bar Code" dialog box.

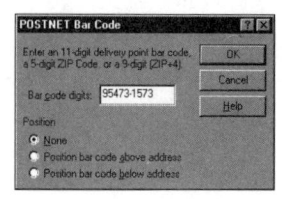

4. Press Enter or click OK.

When you return to your document, you see the weird bar code characters in the document.

> **TIP**
> You can add POSTNET bar codes to envelopes when you're addressing them with the Envelope feature (see the "Envelope" section in Part IV).

Character Map

You can use a character map to reduce document size when you edit documents in non-Roman alphabets such as Greek, Cyrillic, or Hebrew. You must have a language module or Corel WordPerfect 9 language package installed before you can set up character mapping. After installing:

1. Choose Tools⇨Language⇨Character Mapping to open the "Document Character Map" dialog box.

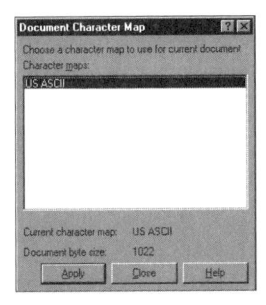

2. Choose a character map from the list box.

3. Click Apply or press Enter.

TIP

To select a character map for all new documents you can do one of the following:

✦ Select the character map in the Current Document Style (see "Styles" in Part III).

✦ Save the selection to the template you use for that language (see "Document" later in this part).

Comments

You can add comments to your text that appear in a text box on your screen but are not printed as part of the document.

Creating a comment

To create a comment, follow these steps:

1. Place the insertion point in the document where you want the comment to be located.

2. Choose Insert⇨Comment⇨Create.

Document

WordPerfect 9 opens the Comment editing window that looks exactly like a document window (you can recognize it by the word "Comment" in parentheses in the title bar) and also calls forth the Comment Property Bar. These are the available options on the Comment Property Bar:

- **Comment Previous:** Go to the previous comment.
- **Comment Next:** Go to the next comment.
- **Initials:** Insert the user's initials into the comment. Choose Tools⇨Settings⇨Environment to configure this option.
- **Name:** Insert the user's name into the comment. Choose Tools⇨Settings⇨Environment to configure this option.
- **Date text:** Insert the current date into the comment.
- **Time:** Insert the current time into the comment.

3. Type the text of your comment in the Comment editing window.

4. Click Close on the Comment Property Bar to insert the comment into the document.

When you create a comment, a comment icon that represents comment text appears in the left margin of the line that contains the comment. The comment icon appears when you view a document in Page or Two Pages mode. You can click the icon to see comment text, double-click to edit the comment, or right-click to select options on the comment QuickMenu.

Editing a comment

To edit a comment, double-click the comment icon or click the comment icon or text balloon with the secondary mouse button and choose Edit from the QuickMenu. After you finish making your changes in the Comment editing window, click Close on the Comment Property Bar.

To get rid of a comment, click the comment icon or comment text balloon with the secondary mouse button and choose Delete from the QuickMenu.

Document

The Document commands on the File menu provide you with powerful tools for comparing and annotating documents, as well as creating master documents. The following is a breakdown of the Document commands and their usage:

- **Compare:** Compare two documents (see "Comparing documents" later in this part).
- **Remove Markings:** Hide changes made in a document (see "Comparing documents" later in this part).
- **Redline Method:** Use a redline in the margin to indicate reviewer or editing changes (see "Comparing documents" later in this part).
- **Review:** Annotate a document or view another reviewer's comments. Annotations are created using the Comment feature (see "Comments" earlier in this part).
- **Subdocument:** Select a file as a subdocument of a master document (see "Master/subdocuments" later in this part).
- **Expand Master:** Expand a master document so that you can edit its subdocuments.
- **Condense Master:** Condense a master document after you're finished editing a subdocument or when you just want to edit the master document.
- **Default Font:** Set the default font for a document style (see "Styles" in Part III).
- **Current Document Style:** Edit the current document style.

Comparing documents

You can compare the current version of a document with an earlier version to see what changes have been made. Deleted text is displayed as strikeout text. Added and moved text is displayed as redline text.

After comparing documents, you can restore the current document to the way it looked before the comparison. You can also remove the deleted (strikeout) text but retain the redline attribute for text that has been added or moved.

Master/subdocuments

A *master document* is a document that contains links to other documents called *subdocuments*.

For example, when writing a book, maintaining several small documents for chapters is easier than writing the book in one large document.

Here's how to create a master document:

1. Open or create the file you want to use as a master document.

178 Document

2. Click where you want to insert a subdocument link.

3. Choose File⇨Document⇨Subdocument to open the "Include Subdocument" dialog box.

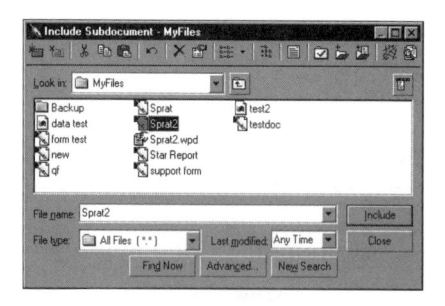

This dialog box, which looks remarkably like an "Open" dialog box, is used to choose a file to link to the master document.

4. Type the filename of a document to link to and then click Include.

5. Repeat Steps 2 through 4 to add other subdocument links.

Here's a list of the things you can do now that you have a master/subdocument link:

✦ Add a title page and table of contents in the master document.

✦ Generate lists or indexes in the master document.

✦ Open, edit, and save subdocuments.

Using a master document

As an example, you can use a master document to generate an index from a number of subdocuments. Here's how:

1. In the subdocuments, mark all the items you want indexed (see "Reference" in Part VI).

2. Expand the master document by choosing File⇨Document⇨Expand Master.

3. Generate the index from the index marks contained in the subdocuments (see "Reference" in Part VI).

The index stays in the master document.

For more information about this feature, see Chapter 17 of *WordPerfect 9 For Windows For Dummies*.

Equation

This tool creates an equation that can be inserted into a document. Here's how to easily finish that report on quantum theory that's due tomorrow:

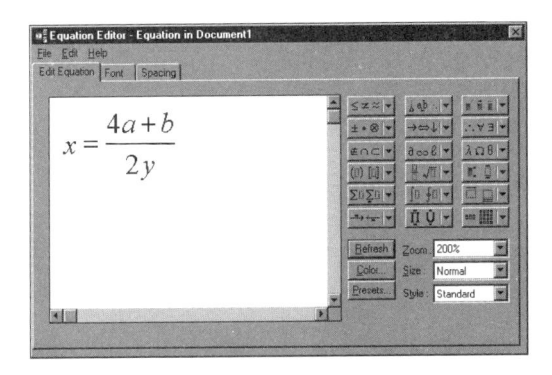

1. Choose Insert⇨Equation to open the "Equation Editor" dialog box.

2. Use the button bar in the "Equation Editor" dialog box to insert mathematical and scientific symbols into your equation.

3. Choose File⇨Exit and Return to Document or click the Close button on the title bar.

Highlight

This tool lets you highlight text by changing the background color.

To use the highlight feature, follow these steps:

1. Select the text you want to highlight.

2. Choose Tools⇨Highlight⇨On.

The selected text is highlighted in the color of choice.

3. If you want to change the highlight color, choose Tools⇨Highlight⇨Color to open the "Highlight Color" dialog box.

Language

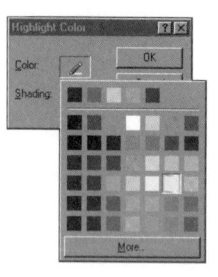

4. Select a color from the Color drop-down palette.

5. Use the Shading scroll list (hidden behind the Color drop-down palette in the figure) to specify the highlight shading percentage.

6. Click OK or press Enter to apply the changes.

> **FAST TRACK** — You can quickly highlight text by pressing the Highlight button on the WordPerfect 9 toolbar. The cursor changes to a tiny highlighting pen, and you simply highlight to your heart's content. Click Highlight again to turn off the feature. You can also change the highlight color via the drop-down button attached to the Highlight button on the WordPerfect 9 toolbar.

Language

WordPerfect 9 lets you use the writing tools in a number of different languages. To use this feature when you're subbing a writing class in Croatia, follow these steps:

1. Choose Tools⇨Language⇨Settings to open the "Language" dialog box.

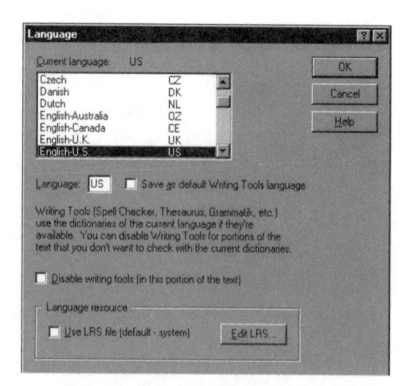

2. Choose from the languages in the Current language list box.

   In the "Language" dialog box, you can choose a default language for the writing tools and choose whether Spell Checker and Grammatik are used under the chosen language dictionary.

   3. Click OK or press Enter to apply your changes.

Master Document

   (See "Document" earlier in this part.)

Paste Special

   You use the Paste Special command to paste elements from other applications into WordPerfect 9. Here's how:

   1. Click to place the insertion point in the spot where you want to place a copy.

   2. Open the application and file from which you want to copy.

   3. Select the information you want to copy to the WordPerfect 9 document and then copy it to the Clipboard by pressing Ctrl+C.

   4. Switch to WordPerfect 9.

   5. Choose Edit⇨Paste Special to open the "Paste Special" dialog box.

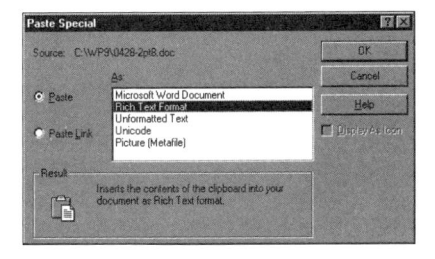

   In the "Paste Special" dialog box, you can choose to paste or link the contents of the Clipboard to the open document.

   6. Click OK or press Enter to finish the Paste Special command.

Reveal Codes

This command opens the Reveal Codes window at the bottom of the document editing window. As you edit and format your text, you can view as well as edit all those wacky secret codes that WordPerfect 9 insists on putting in your document.

Revealing the codes

To view the secret codes in the document, choose View⇨Reveal Codes or press Alt+F3.

[FAST TRACK] You may find that the quicker approach is to open the Reveal Codes window with the mouse. Position the mouse pointer on the rectangular button on the bottom of the vertical scroll bar. When the pointer becomes a double-headed arrow, drag the mouse up or down until the Reveal Codes window is where you want it. Then release the mouse button.

To close the Reveal Codes window with the mouse, position the mouse pointer somewhere on the border between the regular document window and the Reveal Codes window. When the pointer becomes an arrow pointing up and down, drag the border all the way up or down until you reach the Property bar or Application bar. Then release the mouse button.

Using Reveal Codes

Reveal Codes gives you a behind-the-scenes look at the placement of the formatting codes that tell your printer how to produce special effects in your document. You can see codes that define new margin settings, define tabs, center and bold lines of text, set larger font sizes for titles and headings, create paragraph borders around your footer text, and so on.

Reveal Codes 183

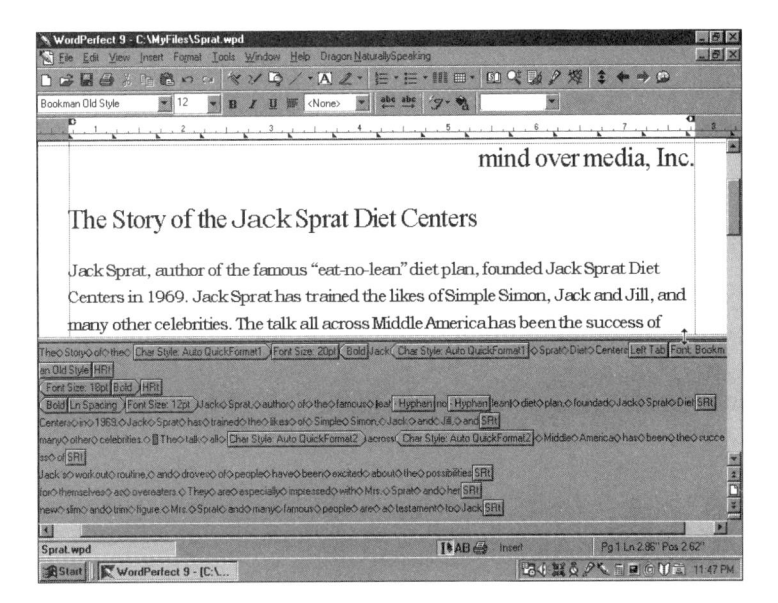

This information is of absolutely no concern to a normal human being, unless, of course, something is wrong with the format of a document and you can't figure how to fix it by using the normal editing window. In that situation, you have to get under the hood, so to speak, by opening the Reveal Codes window. Then you can edit with all those little secret codes in full view.

When you're editing with the Reveal Codes window open, use the regular document editing window above it to find your general place in the document. Then concentrate on what's happening in the Reveal Codes window to make your changes. You can use the mouse to reposition the Reveal Codes cursor in the Reveal Codes window by simply clicking the mouse pointer where you want it to be. (It's not really an insertion point in this window because it appears as a red block.)

To delete a code, use the Delete or Backspace key, depending on where you position the insertion point. You can also remove a code by selecting it and then dragging it until the pointer is outside the Reveal Codes window. Then release the mouse button.

Removing a secret code cancels the associated command or function. Therefore, Reveal Codes is a great tool for zapping pesky formatting problems in a document.

For more information about this command, see Chapter 10 of *WordPerfect 9 For Windows For Dummies*.

Sound

You can insert digital (.wav) and MIDI sound files into a document. Sounds can be used to enhance the document by adding sound effects, music, and voice recordings. You need a sound card and microphone or other input device (for recording your own sounds).

What's that sound?

To add or create sound-enhanced documents, follow these steps:

1. Choose Insert⇨Sound to open the "Sound Clips" dialog box.

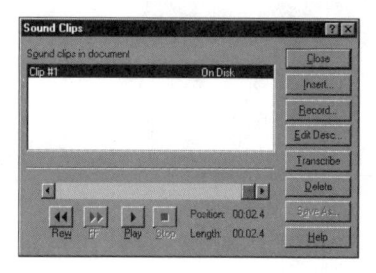

2. Choose from the following options:

- **Sound clips in document:** Lists all the sound clips that have been inserted in the document.

- **Insert:** Adds a sound clip to your document after selecting one in the Sound clips in document window.

- **Record:** Records a sound clip using Microsoft Sound Recorder.

- **Edit Desc:** Names that sound clip.

- **Transcribe:** Displays the Sound Clip Property Bar when sound clips are listed in the document. Works just like your CD player controls. The same controls are available in the "Sound Clips" dialog box.

- **Delete:** Deletes the sound clip from the document.

Recording a sound

1. Click Record in the "Sound Clips" dialog box to open the Microsoft Sound Recorder.

Sound

2. Record the sound, using a microphone or other input device.

3. Save the sound by choosing File⇨Save As.

4. Close the Sound Recorder either using the Close button or File⇨Exit.

> **TIP:** Sound is recorded by using the Microsoft Sound Recorder. Refer to your Windows documentation for more information.

Adding a sound clip to your document

1. Open the "Sound Clips" dialog box.

2. Click Insert to open the "Insert Sound Clip into Document" dialog box.

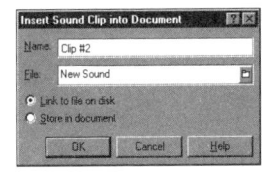

3. Type a descriptive name for the sound clip in the Name text box.

4. In the File text box, type the filename of the sound file to be inserted.

5. Select whether to link the sound file (the sound is a separate file), or store it in the document (the file is part of the document, making the document size larger).

6. Click OK or press Enter to insert the sound clip into the document.

To play the inserted sound clip, just click the speaker icon in the left margin of the document.

Spreadsheet/Database

You can import and link information from a spreadsheet file or a database file into a WordPerfect 9 document.

When you import a spreadsheet or database, the information is copied from the spreadsheet or database in a static state, meaning what you see is what you get. When you link spreadsheet or database information, you can update the information in your document to reflect changes in the original file.

To import static spreadsheet or database information, follow these steps:

1. Click to place the insertion point where you want the imported data.

2. Choose Insert⇨Spreadsheet/Database⇨Import to open the "Import Data" dialog box.

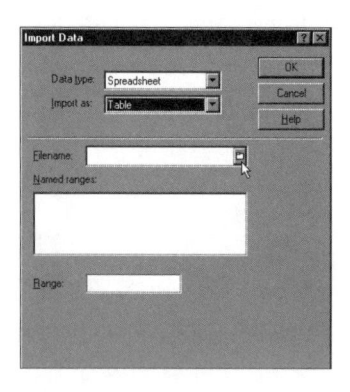

3. Define the import process with the following options:

   - **Data type:** Choose Spreadsheet or a type of database for the imported object from the drop-down list.

   - **Import as:** Select to import the information as text, a table structure, or a merge data file.

   - **Filename:** Type the name of the file or use the browse button to find the file to import.

   - **Named ranges:** Specify a named range in the spreadsheet/database to import or link to.

   - **Range:** Specify a cell range to import or link to.

4. After you finish defining the import operation, click OK or press Enter to insert the information into the current document.

5. To link spreadsheet/database information that can be updated to reflect changes in the spreadsheet/database file, choose Insert➪Spreadsheet/Database➪Create Link to open the "Create Data Link" dialog box, which looks and functions exactly like the "Import Data" dialog box.

6. Define the link operation.

7. Click OK or press Enter to insert the data link in the current document.

> **TIP:** If you are importing or linking to an SQL (Structured Query Language) database, you must log on to the database server.

WordPerfect Office 2000

WordPerfect 9 is one part of a group of powerful programs called Corel WordPerfect Office 2000.

How suite it is

When you install WordPerfect Office 2000, you are given the choice of installing the following programs:

- **Corel WordPerfect 9:** The powerful word-processing program and reason for this book
- **Corel Quattro Pro 9:** A feature-rich spreadsheet program
- **Corel Presentations 9:** An easy-to-use presentation program for creating drawings and slide shows
- **CorelCENTRAL 9:** An integrated PIM or Personal Information Manager that includes a calendar, memos, address book, and contacts
- **CorelCENTRAL Address Book:** Quick access to the CorelCENTRAL Address Book
- **Paradox 9:** A powerful and easy-to-use relational database program

Using WordPerfect Office 2000

The Corel programs share many of the same features that make WordPerfect 9 so easy to use, like Property bars, the PerfectExpert, and the Internet Publisher. You can also access each of these programs quickly by using the Desktop Applications Director (DAD).

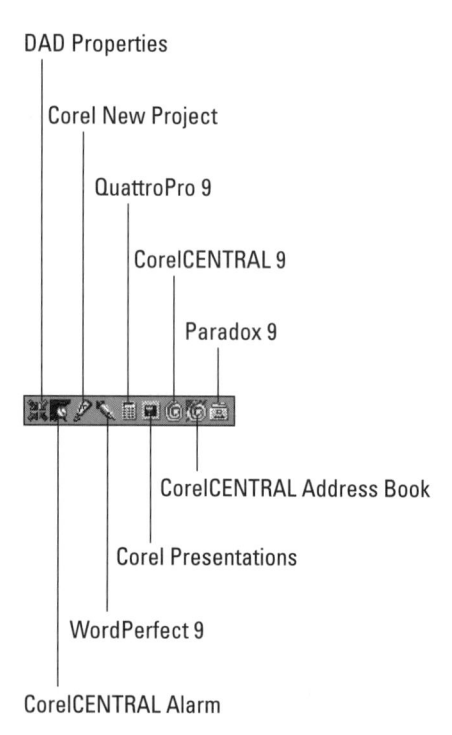

WordPerfect Office 2000

DAD Properties

Corel New Project

QuattroPro 9

CorelCENTRAL 9

Paradox 9

CorelCENTRAL Address Book

Corel Presentations

WordPerfect 9

CorelCENTRAL Alarm

To open and switch between programs via DAD, just click the program icon on the Desktop Applications Director toolbar.

Techie Talk

advance: Normally, what brightens an author's day. In WordPerfect 9, however, it's the ability to move, or advance, a text block to any place in the page.

cell: The box formed at the intersection of a row and a column in a table. Like its counterpart in the human body, a table's smallest component.

check box: A little box in a dialog box that you put a check mark in to select the option.

click: To press the primary or secondary mouse button. Named for the sound it makes unless your mouse is *very* dirty.

clip art: Little (see also *sizing handles*) graphics and pictures you can insert into your documents to liven things up. In the old days, you would clip these goodies out of books and paste them on a board with your text, and take a photo of the board, and well, you get the picture.

Clipboard: The Clipboard stores the text and graphics you want to copy or move until you decide where you want to paste them.

cursor: The on-screen symbol with many faces (blinking insertion point, I-beam, arrow pointer, and so on) whose main function is to ape your mouse movements so you can tell where you are in the document window.

dialog box: A box that shows up when the computer needs more input to perform a command. You fill in the needed info and click OK to start the task. Despite its name, the dialog box is not a scintillating conversationalist. See also *check box, drop-down list,* and *radio button.*

document: You may call it a letter, legal brief, screenplay, or memo, but to WordPerfect 9, it is and will always be a document.

double-click: (see *click*) Twice.

drop-down list: A menu box with a little down arrow control that, when clicked, causes its contents to pour forth for selection purposes.

field: A place in a document reserved for variable data. Great for mail merges (see "Merge" in Part IV). When you want to write a thank-you note to all the people in your My Fans database, put a *Fan's Name* field in the letter (preferably after *Dear* in the salutation) and then merge the letter with the database, and like magic, generate a letter for each and every fan.

file extension: The three-character extension following the period in a Windows filename that varies among programs. WordPerfect 9 uses .wpd for its files. From DOS to Windows 98, it remains a reason for much smugness in the Macintosh community.

font: A specific (in size and attributes) typeface design.

fontina: A type of Italian cheese, semi-soft to firm, made of ewe's milk.

footer: A small area in the bottom margin of a document reserved for information like the document's title, page number, date, and shoe size. See also *header*.

function keys: The numbered keys that start with the letter F (I know that it's a contradiction) on the keyboard; they perform certain commands quickly.

graphics line: Those perky singing and dancing graphics in a Broadway show. Or a line you can format in all sorts of ways to enrich your document. You decide.

header: A small area in the top margin of a document reserved for information like the document's title, page number, date, and hat size. See also *footer*.

HTML: HyperText Markup Language. The language that has caused everyone to scratch their heads and say, "What's all this I hear about a World Wide Web?" Documents in WordPerfect 9 can be converted to HTML so that they can be viewed in an Internet browser like Netscape Navigator.

hyperlink: Not a young link that's had too much chocolate before bedtime, but a dynamic spot in your document that, when clicked, transports you to another place entirely. That place can be in the current document, in another file, on an intranet, or anywhere on the Internet.

independent front suspension: Just wanted another entry that starts with the letter I.

Internet: The vast network of computers set up by the government in the Cold War years to hook up educational and military research facilities. Today, it's the home of the World Wide Web.

intranet: Often confused with its big brother (see also *Internet*). You create an intranet anytime you set up a host computer or server that can be accessed via a Web browser by other computers.

justification: Why am I here? Oh yeah, to tell you that justification in word-processing lingo is basically about whether text lines up on the left margin, the right margin, or dead on center.

kerning: To alter the space between two or more adjacent letters. Also what a cocktail pianist is doing when playing a Jerome Kern medley.

keyboard shortcuts: Key combinations the mousaphobe can use to do menu commands. By the way, they are usually the quicker way to go.

leading: The vertical distance between two lines of type. A throwback to the days when lines of type on a printing plate were separated by thin strips of lead.

margin: The space between the four edges of a page and the text within. Also, what the CEO of Corel hopes to increase with sales of WordPerfect 9.

mouse: Right up there with Mickey in the *rodents as cultural icons* category. You use it to move the cursor around the screen.

orphan: The hero in a Victorian tale about a lonely first line of a paragraph that gets left behind at the bottom of a page while the rest of its buddies run merrily off to the top of the next page. WordPerfect 9, like most word-processors, features a way of stopping this tragic scenario.

overstrike: Once upon a time, if you wanted to type a divided by (÷) symbol in a math equation, you had to type a colon and then backspace and overstrike the colon with a dash. Given all the iconic, scientific, mathematics, and International symbols available for inserting into a document in WordPerfect 9, I'm hard pressed to find any modern-day usefulness for this feature. E-mail me if you find one.

paste: Yuck! My brothers used to eat this stuff after school. When you copy or move something in a document, the last thing you want to do is paste it in a new location.

point: Although your mother always told you not to, in the computer world, you can do it (with the mouse that is) until the cows come home.

Property bar: The spiffy, context-sensitive toolbar in WordPerfect 9 that sits right above the document window and magically provides the basic tools needed for the task at hand. See also *toolbar*.

QuickCorrect: A WordPerfect 9 feature that automatically corrects commonly misspelled words. It can even be taught to correct words you commonly misspell due to sloppy typing. A nice feature, though I'm not sure that Mavis Beacon would approve.

QuickWords: Another great WordPerfect 9 feature that lets you create abbreviations for long phrases. When you type the abbreviation, WordPerfect 9 completes the longer phrase assigned to it. Great for typing URLs or other phrases where accuracy is paramount.

radio button: One of a group of two or more small round buttons that appear in a dialog box. They are used for selecting specific options because you can only select one from the group.

save: The work you do in the WordPerfect 9 document window is not permanently stored until you save it to the hard drive, a floppy, or other storage media. Do yourself a favor and become one with this little mantra: *Save often.*

scroll: To move up, down, or sideways through a document using the horizontal and vertical scroll bars on the right side and bottom of the document window. If the Egyptians had scroll bars, would books have been invented?

sizing handles: Eight little black squares that form a frame around a graphic inserted into a document. You have to select the graphic for these to show up. When you float the cursor over a sizing handle, the cursor turns into a multi-headed arrow pointer that indicates the direction you can drag the handle to enlarge or reduce the size of the graphic.

sort: WordPerfect 9 lets you arrange a list alphabetically or numerically. When sorting alphabetically, you can choose to sort by the first word or line in a paragraph.

style: When you set up specific attributes for a font, line, paragraph, and so on, you are creating a style. After it's defined, you can apply this style to selected text and bypass the rigmarole of choosing all the attributes in the Font dialog box. Used to format headings, paragraphs, lists, and so forth on the fly.

template: Pre-formatted documents with customized content and features. For example, WordPerfect 9 includes a fax cover sheet template that's set up so you only have to fill in your personal information and save it under a new name. Dozens of templates in various categories are installed in WordPerfect 9.

TextArt: A WordPerfect 9 application that changes words in your documents into designs. You can shape the image using patterns, colors, and other options, or you can select from a wide variety of pre-designed 2-D and 3-D shapes.

toolbar: A bar containing a number of buttons, drop-down lists, and menus. It offers one-click access to just about every command available in WordPerfect 9. See also *Property bar.*

watermark: A printable image or graphic placed behind the text in a document. Vary the shade of the watermark to enhance text visibility. Real watermarks are pressed into the paper and are visible only when held up to the light.

widow: A variation on the tragic orphan story (see also *orphan*) where the heroine is a very short line of text (like one word) that is left all alone at the end of a paragraph in a sea of white space. As always, WordPerfect 9 comes to the rescue.

WordPerfect 9 toolbar: The main toolbar in WordPerfect 9 that sits right below the menu bar and contains some of the more basic tools used in day to day tasks. See also *toolbar.*

Index

A

Action option, on find and replace dialog box, 28
active window, 55
Add Visual Elements option, PerfectExpert, 44
Address Book, 172–174
address labels, formatting, 91–93
Advance, typesetting, 138
advancing text blocks, 189
alignment, 76
  centered text, 64
  flush right, 69–70
  indents, 67–68
  justification, 191
  Property bar, 123
Alt key, 9
Append command, Clipboard and, 25
Application bar, 16, 106–107
arrow keys
  insertion point, moving, 37
  keyboard location, 8
arrows, shapes and, 149
Ask the PerfectExpert, Help, 34
Auto Scroll, 107–108
automatic line height, 143

B

background fills, creating, 22–23
Backspace key, deleting text, 26
bar code, 174
bars, hiding, 116–117
block protect, Keep Text Together, 138, 142
blocks, text, extending, 51–52
bold text, 62, 123
Bookmark dialog box, 108–109
bookmarks
  creating, 108–109
  finding, 109
  hyperlinks, 158
Border/Fill option, 22–23
borders, 22–23
  drop caps, 69
  pages, 41
  paragraphs, 43
boxes, graphics, 138–141
breaking pages, 42
Browse button, 16
browsers, viewing Web documents, 165
bullets, 62–64, 79
Bullets and Numbering dialog box, 62
busy cursor, 7
buttons
  dialog boxes, 14
  mouse, 9
  palettes, PerfectExpert, 45
  Property bar, 122–123
  Redo, 54
  toolbars, 134–135
  Undo, 54

C

callouts, shapes, 150
Cancel command, 23
canceling actions, 23
Caps Lock key, 9
cascading windows, 55
cells, tables, 189
Center Pages dialog box, 64–65
centering
  page, 64–65
  text, 64

character maps, 175
characters, WordPerfect, 87–88
check boxes, dialog boxes, 14, 189
clicking mouse buttons, 10, 189
clipart, 139, 189
Clipboard, 25, 189
Close command, 23
closing documents, 23
codes
  Reveal Codes, 182–183
  viewing, 52–53
color
  fonts, 71
  highlighted text, 179–180
  hyperlinks, 158–159
  Internet Publisher, 162
columns
  creating, 65–66
  moving through, 66–67
  tables, 152
Columns dialog box, 65–66
commands
  NaturallySpeaking, 115
  selecting from menu, 11
  shortcut keys, 11–12
comments, 175–176
comparing documents, 177
conditional end of page, Keep Text Together, 138, 142
Contents, Help, 34
context-sensitive help, 34–35
Control menu, main screen, 15
Convert File Format dialog box, 41
copies, printing, 102
Copy command, 24–25
copying text, mouse, 27
Corel PerfectExpert dialog box, 44
CorelCENTRAL 9, 187
CorelCENTRAL Address Book, 172–174, 187
Covert Case command, 24
creation date, document summary, 46
cross references, 146
Ctrl key, 8
cursors, 6–7
  busy cursor, 7
  defined, 189
  Help cursor, 7
  hourglass cursor, 7
  insertion point, 7, 37
  mouse cursor, 7
  shadow cursor, 133
Cut command, 24–25

D

DAD (Desktop Applications Director), 18–19
  adding program icons to, 110
  editing QuickTips, 111
  getting rid of, 110-111
  starting, 111
  WordPerfect Office 2000, 187
data files, merges, 93–96
databases, 186–187
date/time, 111–112
Delete key, 8
deleting
  NaturallySpeaking, 115
  text, 25–26
desktop publishing, 137–156
  adding shapes, 149-150
  inserting and editing graphics, 138-142
  Keep Text Together dialog box, 142
  line height, 143
  Make It Fit dialog box, 144-145
  marking text to create lists, 146-149
  Paragraph Format dialog box, 145
  sorting text, 150-152
  tables, 152-154
  watermarks, 155-156
dialog boxes
  buttons, 14
  canceling, 23
  check boxes, 14
  defined, 189
  drop-down lists, 14

radio buttons, 192
scroll lists, 14
dictating with NaturallySpeaking, 113
Document commands, File menu, 176–178
Document Information. *See* properties
document list, Reference menu, 148–149
Document Summary. *See also* properties, 46
document window
  defined, 16
  editing labels in, 93
Document1, 6
documents, 190
  closing, 23
  comparing, 177
  converting to Web page, 166–167
  defined, 6
  master, 177–178
  naming, 6
  new, 6, 38–40
  opening, 40–41
  saving, 6
  sound clips, 185
  starting, 38–40
  subdocuments, 177–178
  templates, 39–40
dot leaders, tabs, 86
double indents, 67–68
Draft view, 26, 43
drag and drop, mouse, 10, 27
Dragon NaturallySpeaking voice recognition software, 112–116
Draw Object Shapes dialog box, 149
drop caps, 68–69
drop shadows, shapes, 150
drop-down lists, 14, 190

E

Edit and Proofread option, PerfectExpert, 45
editing
  comments, 176
  document summaries, 47
  footnote/endnote text, 30
  graphics, 141
  hyperlinks, 159
embedded fonts, 49
End key, 8
endnotes. *See* footnotes and endnotes
Enhanced Password Protection, 48
Enter key, 8, 17
envelopes
  bar code, 174
  merges and, 99
  printing, 90–91
equations, 179
Esc key, 7
Exit command, 27
exiting WordPerfect 9, 27

F

Face option, Font Properties dialog box, 71
features, Property bar, 123–124
fields, merge data files, 94–95, 190
file extensions, 190
file formats, 41
File name option, Open File dialog box, 41
File type option, Open File dialog box, 41
filenames
  document summary, properties, 46
  extensions, 190
  headers/footers, 91
  inserting in documents, 91
  macros, 118

files
  form files, merges, 96–98
  passwords, 48
  saving, 47–49
filling areas, 22–23
find and replace, 27–29
Find and Replace dialog box, 28
Find Now option, Open File dialog box, 41
Finish option, PerfectExpert, 45
fixed line height, 143
floating cells, tables, 152
flowchart, 150
flush right alignment, 69–70
Font Properties dialog box, 70–72
fonts, 70–74, 190
  color, 71
  drop caps, 69
  embedded, 49
  Internet Publisher, 162
  Make It Fit, 144
  page numbering, 43
  Property bar, 122
  RealTime Preview, 73–74
  toolbars, 135
footers. *See* headers and footers
Footnote/Endnote dialog box, 29–30
footnotes and endnotes, 29–31
  editing text, 30
  numbering, 30–31
foreign languages, character map, 175
form files, merges, 96–98
formats, file formats, 41
formatting
  alignment, 69–70
  bold type, 62
  bullets, 62–64
  centering, 64–65
  columns, 65–67
  drop caps, 68–69
  fonts, 70–74
  indents, 67–68, 74–76
  Insert mode, 87
  justification, 76
  line numbering, 76–77
  margins, 78
  NaturallySpeaking, 115
  numbered lists, 62–64
  outlines, 78–81
  page numbering, 43
  paragraph format, 145–146
  PerfectExpert, 44
  QuickFormat, 129–130
  redline text, 72, 81
  Ruler bar, 82–83
  strikeout text, 72, 81
  styles, 83–85
  tables, SpeedFormat, 152
  tabs, 85–87
  Typeover mode, 87
  underlined text, 87
forms, Web pages, 164–165
frames, 138
function keys, 7, 190

G

Go To, 116
  bookmarks, 109
grammar checker, Prompt-As-You-Go, 121
Grammar-As-You-Go. *See also* Proofread, 116, 121
Grammatik, 31, 55, 57–59. *See also* Writing Tools
graphics, 138–141
  inserting in documents, 139
  watermarks, 156
  Web pages, 162
graphics lines, 190
guidelines, margins, 142

H

hanging indents, 74–75
hard page breaks, 42
Header/Footer dialog box, 32

headers and footers, 31–33, 190
Help cursor, 7
Help, 33–35. *See also* PerfectExpert
highlighting text, 179–180
Home key, 8
hot zone, hyphenation, 36
hourglass cursor, 7
HTML, 160, 190
HTML Table Format dialog box, 163
hyperlinks, 158–160, 190
hyphenation, 35–36
  positioning hyphen, 36

I

icons
  comment, 166
  Desktop Applications Director
    (DAD) 18-19, 110-111
  margin, 82
  used in this book, 3
importing spreadsheet or database
    information, 186-187
indents, 75–76
  double, 67–68
  hanging indents, 74–75
  paragraph formatting, 145
  Ruler bar, 82
Index, Help, 34
indexes, 146
Information option, properties, 47
Insert key, 8
Insert mode, 87
insertion point, 7, 37
  mouse pointer comparison, 37
  recording macros, 117
Internet
  defined, 191
  Web publishing on, 157–169
Internet Publisher, 160–168
intranets, 191
italic text, Property bar, 123

J

justification, 64, 76, 191
  flush right, 69–70
  Property bar, 123

K

Keep Text Together, 142–143
kerning, typesetting, 155, 191
keyboard, 7–9
  Alt key, 9
  arrow keys, 8
  Caps Lock key, 9
  Ctrl key, 8
  Delete key, 8
  End key, 8
  Enter key, 8
  Esc key, 7
  function keys, 7
  Home key, 8
  Insert key, 8
  insertion point, moving, 37
  Num Lock key, 8
  Page Down key, 8
  Page Up key, 8
  Pause key, 7
  Print Screen key, 7
  Scroll Lock key, 7
  Shift key, 9
  shortcut keys, 11–12, 191
  text selection, 51–52

L

labels
  creating and editing, 91–93
  merges and, 99
languages, 180–181
leaders, tabs, 86
leading, spacing, 191
line height, 143–144

Line Hyphenation dialog box, 35
line numbering, 76–77
line spacing
  changing, 38
  Make It Fit, 145
Line Spacing dialog box, 35
lines
  graphics, 190
  rules, 164
  shapes and, 149
  sorting by, 151
links, hyperlinks, 158–160
list definition, Reference menu, 147
lists, adding to Web pages, 163–164
Look in option, Open File dialog box, 41
lowercase, converting to/from upper, 24

M

macros
  playing back, 119
  recording, 117–118
  templates, attaching to, 119–120
mail merges. *See* merges
mailings, label printing, 91–93
main screen
  application bar, 16
  Browse button, 16
  Control menu, 15
  document window, 16
Make It Fit, 144–145
margin lines, 16
margins. *See also* alignment, 78, 191
  flush right, 69–70
  guidelines, 142
  hyphenation and, 35–36
  lines, 16
  paragraph formatting, 146
  Ruler bar, 82
  tabs, 86
master documents, 177–178
Match option, find and replace, 28
math symbols, 179

menu bar, 16
  hiding, 116–117
  Next button, 16
  Previous button, 16
  ruler, 16
  scoll bars, 16
  Title bar, 15
  windows, sizing, 16
  WordPerfect 9 toolbar, 16
  WordPerfect menu bar, 16
menus, 10–14
  commands, selecting, 11
  Control menu, 15
  Quick Tips, 11
  QuickMenus, 9, 12–13, 130
  Reference menu, 146–149
Merge dialog box, 94–96
merges
  data files, 93–96
  fields, 190
  performing, 98–99
Microsoft Internet Explorer, 160
Microsoft Sound Recorder, 184-185
MIDI sound files, 184
Minimize button, 15-16
mouse, 10–11, 191
  buttons, 9
  clicking techniques, 10
  copying text, 27
  cursor, 7
  drag and drop, 10, 27
  insertion point, moving, 37
  macro recording, 120
  text, selecting, 51
mouse pointer
  insertion point comparison, 37
  toolbars and, 134
moving
  graphics, 141
  insertion point, 37
  text, 24–25
  text, mouse, 27
  through columns, 66–67
  toolbars, 134
  versus copying, 24–25

Index

N

naming documents, 6
navigation, NaturallySpeaking, 115
Netscape Navigator, 160
new documents, 6, 38–40
Next button, 16
Num Lock key, 8
numbered lists, 62–64
numbering
　footnotes/endnotes, 30–31
　headers/footers, 32
　line numbering, 76–77
　pages, 42–43

O

Open command, 40–41
Open File dialog box, 40–41
opening documents, 38–41
Options option, find and replace, 28
Original Password Protection, 48
orphans, 142, 191
Outline Property Bar, 80–81
outlines, 78–81. *See also* bullets
overstrike text, 191

P

page borders, 41
page breaks, 42
page centering, 64–65
Page Down key, 8
page numbering, 42
　tabs, 86
　toolbars, 135
page numbers
　adding, 42–43
　Go To and, 116
Page Setup dialog box, 99–100
page size, 99–100
Page Up key, 8
Page view, 43
palettes, PerfectExpert, 45
Paradox 9, 187
paragraph formatting, 145–146
paragraph symbols, viewing, 17
paragraphs, 17
　aligning, 76
　borders, 43
　borders on, 23
　double indenting, 67–68
　indenting, 75–76
　starting a new paragraph, 17
　styles, 85
password protection, 48
Paste command, 24–25
pasting, 191
paste special, 181
Pause key, 7
PerfectExpert, 44–45
　Internet Publisher, 161
　templates, dialog box, 39–40
playing macros, 119
pointing, 191
position
　drop caps, 69
　fonts, 71
　hyphens, 36
POSTNET (Postal Numeric Encoding Technique), 174
Presentations 9, 187
previews, RealTime Preview, 73–74
Previous button, 16
primary mouse button, 9
Print dialog box, 101–103
Print Screen key, 7
printer, selecting, 101–102
printing
　Application bar, 106
　envelopes, 90–91
　labels, 91–93
　page size and, 99–100
program icons, DAD and, 18
Prompt-As-You-Go
Proofread, 120–122
properties, 45–47
　hyperlinks, 158
　printing, 102

Property bar, 16, 192
  adding features, 123-124
  buttons, 122-123
pull-down menus
  canceling, 23
  opening, 10

Q

Quattro Pro 9, 187
Quick Tips, menus, 11
QuickCorrect, 125–126, 192
QuickFind button, Property
    bar, 123
QuickFinder, 126–129
QuickFormat, 129–130
QuickMarks, 108, 109
QuickMenus, 12–13, 130
  Graphics QuickMenu, 139
  secondary mouse button, 9
  text, selecting, 51
QuickStyle, 83–84
QuickTips, 35
QuickWords, 130–132, 192
quitting WordPerfect, 27

R

radio buttons, 192
RealTime Preview, fonts, 73–74
Record Macro dialog box, 118
recording macros, 117–118
recording sound, 184–185
records, merge data files, 95–96
redline text, 72, 81, 177
Redo button, 54
Reference menu, 146–149
repeating characters, 132–133
Replace option, find and
    replace, 28
replacing text. *See* find and replace
resolution area, printing, 102
Restore button, 15–16

return address, envelopes, 90
Reveal Codes, 182–183
revision date, document
    summary, 46
rows, tables, 152
ruler, 16
Ruler bar
  hiding, 116–117
  using, 82–83
rules, Web pages, 164

S

Save As, 49–50
Save As dialog box, 50
Save File dialog box, 6, 47–48
Save User File button,
    NaturallySpeaking, 113
saving, 47–49, 192
  documents, 6
  documents converted to Web
      pages, 167–168
  embedded fonts, 49
  files, 47–49
scientific symbols, 179
Scrapbook, 139
screen
  cursors, 6–7
  main screen, 14–16
scroll bars, 16, 135
scroll lists, 14
Scroll Lock key, 7
scrolling
  Auto Scroll, 107–108
  defined, 192
Search for New Words,
    NaturallySpeaking, 113
searches, QuickFinder, 126–129
secondary mouse button, 9
selecting
  NaturallySpeaking, 115
  text, 51–52
  text, blocks, 51–52

Index

Set Up the Document option, PerfectExpert, 44
Settings dialog box, 52–53
shading, 22, 71
shadow cursor, 133
Shadow cursor, Application bar, 106
shadows, 22
shapes, 149–150
Shift key, 9
shortcut keys, 11–12, 191
  copying/cutting/pasting, 24–25
  find and replace operations, 29
  text selection, 51–52
Show command, 52–53
size
  fonts, 71
  graphics, 141
  handlines, 192
sizing handles, 192
sizing windows, 16
skewing table cells, 153–154
sorts, 150–152, 192
sound, 184–185
Sound Clips dialog box, 184
spacing
  columns, 66
  dot leaders, tabs, 86
  kerning, 191
  leading, 191
  line height and, 143–144
  line spacing, 38
  paragraph formatting, 146
SpeedFormat, tables, 152
SpeedLinks, hyperlinks, 159–160
Spell Check, 53, 55, 56–57. *See also* Writing Tools
Spell-As-You-Go, 121
spell checker, Prompt-As-You-Go, 121
spreadsheets, 186–187
stars, shapes and, 150
Start option, PerfectExpert, 44
starting WordPerfect 9, 17–19
Status bar, 134. *See also* Application bar
  hiding, 116–117

stock text, abbreviations for, 130–132
strikeout text, 72, 81
styles, 83–85, 192
  boxes, graphics, 139–141
  dialog boxes, 83–84
  graphics, boxes, 139–141
subdocuments, 177–178
Summary option, properties, 46–47
symbols
  codes, viewing, 52–53
  WordPerfect characters, 87–88
synonyms. *See* Thesaurus

T

Tab Set dialog box, 85–86
Table of Authorities, 146
Table of Contents, 146
Table QuickCreate button, WordPerfect 9 toolbar, 153
tables, 152–154
  cells, 189
  merge data files, 93–96
  Web pages, 163
tabs
  on the Ruler bar, 82–83
  setting, 85–87
taskbar, adding/removing items, 18
templates, 192
  macros, attaching, 119–120
  selecting, 39–40
text
  blocks, advancing, 189
  blocks, extending, 51–52
  bold, 62
  centering, 64
  copying, 24–25
  cutting, 24–25
  date as, 111–112
  deleting, 25–26
  drag and drop, 27
  entering in tables, 153
  highlighting, 179–180
  Keep Text Together, 142–143

text *(continued)*
  pasting, 24–25
  QuickWords, 130–132
  repeating characters, 132
  selecting, 51–52
Text Property bar, 122
text underlined, 87
TextArt, 139, 193
thesaurus, Prompt-As-You-Go, 121
Thesaurus, 53, 55, 59–60. *See also* Writing Tools
tiling windows, 55
Tip option, PerfectExpert, 45
Title bar, main screen, 15
toolbars, 134–136, 193
  Application bar, 16, 106–107
  hiding, 116–117
  Outline Property Bar, 80–81
  Property bar, 16, 122–124
  WordPerfect 9, 16
Train a Word or Phrase, NaturallySpeaking, 113, 114
Turn Microphone On/Off, NaturallySpeaking, 113
Two Page view, 53
Type option, find and replace, 28
Typeover mode, 87
typesetting, 155
Typing option, PerfectExpert, 44
typing, styles and, 84–85
typos, QuickCorrect, 125–126

U

underlined text, 87, 123
Undo, 26, 54
Undo button, 54
Undo/Redo History dialog box, 54
uppercase, converting to/from lower, 24
Use NaturalWord button, NaturallySpeaking, 113

V

viewing code symbols, 52–53
views
  Draft view, 26, 43
  Page view, 43
  Two Page, 53
  Web Page, 168–169
visual elements, PerfectExpert, 44
voice recognition software, 112–116

W

watermarks, 33, 193
  creating, 155–156
  Draft view and, 26
Web Page view, 168–169
Web pages
  converting documents to, 166–167
  creating, 161–162
  forms, 164–165
  graphics, 162
  lists, 163–164
  tables, 163
  viewing in browser, 165
Web publishing, 157–169
  Internet publishing, 160–168
What's This? icon, 35
white space, hyphenation and, 35–36
widows, 142, 193
windows. *See also* main screen, 55
  active, 55
  cascading, 55
  document window, 16
  sizing, 16
  tiling, 55
WordPerfect 9
  exiting, 27
  menu bar, 16
  starting, 17–19
  toolbar, 16

WordPerfect 9 For Windows For Dummies, 23
WordPerfect 9 toolbar, 193
WordPerfect character symbols, 87–88
WordPerfect Office 2000, 187–188
words, sorting by, 151
Write a Draft option, PerfectExpert, 44
Writing Tools, 55–60
  for different languages, 180-181
  Grammatik, 57-59
  Spell Check, 56-57
  Thesaurus, 59-60
Writing Tools dialog box, 56

X–Y–Z

zooming, 53, 60

Notes

WWW.DUMMIES.COM

Discover Dummies™ Online!

The *Dummies* Web Site is your fun and friendly online resource for the latest information about ...*For Dummies*® books on all your favorite topics. From cars to computers, wine to Windows, and investing to the Internet, we've got a shelf full of ...*For Dummies* books waiting for you!

Ten Fun and Useful Things You Can Do at www.dummies.com

1. Register this book and win!
2. Find and buy the ...*For Dummies* books you want online.
3. Get ten great *Dummies Tips*™ every week.
4. Chat with your favorite ...*For Dummies* authors.
5. Subscribe free to *The Dummies Dispatch*™ newsletter.
6. Enter our sweepstakes and win cool stuff.
7. Send a free cartoon postcard to a friend.
8. Download free software.
9. Sample a book before you buy.
10. Talk to us. Make comments, ask questions, and get answers!

Jump online to these ten fun and useful things at
http://www.dummies.com/10useful

For other technology titles from IDG Books Worldwide, go to
www.idgbooks.com

Not online yet? It's easy to get started with *The Internet For Dummies*,® 5th Edition, or *Dummies 101*®: *The Internet For Windows*® 98, available at local retailers everywhere.

Find other ...*For Dummies* books on these topics:
Business • Careers • Databases • Food & Beverages • Games • Gardening • Graphics
Hardware • Health & Fitness • Internet and the World Wide Web • Networking • Office Suites
Operating Systems • Personal Finance • Pets • Programming • Recreation • Sports
Spreadsheets • Teacher Resources • Test Prep • Word Processing

The IDG Books Worldwide logo is a registered trademark under exclusive license to IDG Books Worldwide, Inc., from International Data Group, Inc. Dummies Tips, the ...For Dummies logo, The Dummies Dispatch, and Dummies are trademarks, and Dummies Man, ...For Dummies, For Dummies, and Dummies 101 are registered trademarks of IDG Books Worldwide, Inc. All other trademarks are the property of their respective owners.

IDG BOOKS WORLDWIDE BOOK REGISTRATION

Register This Book and Win!

We want to hear from you!

Visit **http://my2cents.dummies.com** to register this book and tell us how you liked it!

- Get entered in our monthly prize giveaway.
- Give us feedback about this book — tell us what you like best, what you like least, or maybe what you'd like to ask the author and us to change!
- Let us know any other ...*For Dummies*® topics that interest you.

Your feedback helps us determine what books to publish, tells us what coverage to add as we revise our books, and lets us know whether we're meeting your needs as a ...*For Dummies* reader. You're our most valuable resource, and what you have to say is important to us!

Not on the Web yet? It's easy to get started with *Dummies 101*®: *The Internet For Windows*® *98* or *The Internet For Dummies*,® 5th Edition, at local retailers everywhere.

Or let us know what you think by sending us a letter at the following address:

...*For Dummies* Book Registration
Dummies Press
7260 Shadeland Station, Suite 100
Indianapolis, IN 46256-3917
Fax 317-596-5498

...FOR DUMMIES™
BESTSELLING BOOK SERIES